Alice, [illegible]

The Case of Alice May Parkinson

Carol Markwell

Kind Regards
Jamie

STEELE ROBERTS
AOTEAROA

to Jennie

With grateful thanks to Brian Easton, Phillip Mann, Colin & Nick Markwell.

A catalogue record for this book is available from the
National Library of New Zealand Cataloguing-in-Publication Data
ISBN 978-1-927242-60-5

Cover: painting by Janice Gill
Production: Stefanie Hester, Emma Wolff

STEELE ROBERTS PUBLISHERS
Box 9321 Wellington, Aotearoa New Zealand
info@SteeleRoberts.co.nz • www.SteeleRoberts.co.nz

Alice, what have you done!

Contents

Part One

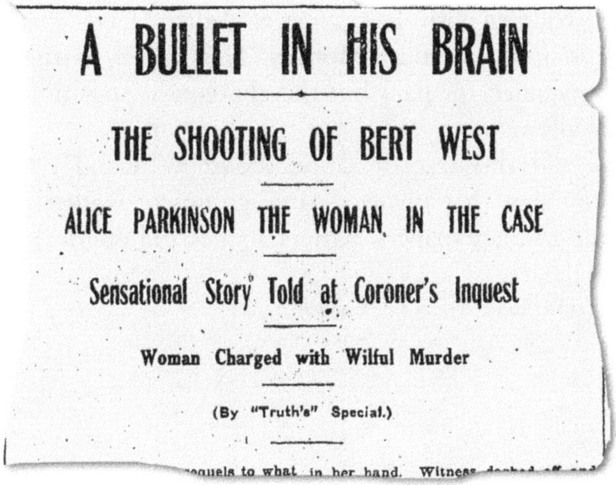

A BULLET IN HIS BRAIN

THE SHOOTING OF BERT WEST

ALICE PARKINSON THE WOMAN IN THE CASE

Sensational Story Told at Coroner's Inquest

Woman Charged with Wilful Murder

(By "Truth's" Special.)

Introduction

These were the headlines in the New Zealand *Truth* on 24 April 1915. The woman in question was Alice May Parkinson, a 25-year-old 'honest, thrifty and hard-working girl' whom 'anyone might be proud of as a friend'.[1] Six weeks earlier in Napier, on the evening of 2 March, Alice had pulled a revolver from her coat pocket and fired at Walter Albert ('Bert') West, a young man she had been going out with. Alice meant business, firing at close range. With the first shot Bert dropped to the ground. She then fired four more times into his prostrate body before turning the revolver on herself and discharging the next bullet into her own head.

Bert West, frothing at the mouth and insensible, with inoperable wounds to the head, chest and neck, lingered on in Napier Hospital before dying three days later on 5 March. Alice, semi-conscious, was also taken to Napier Hospital and, although badly hurt from her self-inflicted wounds, made a slow recovery.

As the 21 April Coroner's inquest in Napier ended, Alice was formally charged with the murder of Walter Albert West and was remanded until the next Monday. Her lawyer, Barney Dolan, formally applied for bail, but the charge was so serious that no bail was allowed.

How did this tragedy come about? Why did it lead to a long campaign that involved large groups of workers, women's organisations, newspapers, writers, judges and political leaders of New Zealand?

And who was Alice Parkinson?

ONE

A bright and cheerful Christian

Alice was born on 29 December 1889 in the Hawke's Bay village of Hampden, and grew up amid a throng of sisters, brothers, grandparents, uncles and aunts.

Alice's father, George Parkinson, had emigrated from Lincolnshire in England with his parents when he was just twelve years old. Alice's mother, Isabella Rosina Beazley, came from Port Levy on Banks Peninsula, Canterbury. Isabella and George probably met in Christchurch, as they were married there in 1881 and their first son, George Henry, was born in Lyttelton a year later, in 1882. Not long after this the young couple shifted to the North Island and moved into a cottage on the corner of Murchison and Mantell Streets in Hampden. The little house would have been crowded, as eleven more children were later born to the family.

George worked as a labourer on Gwavas Station, a big cattle and sheep farm near Hampden. The station was a major local employer, especially in the shearing season. George had been a drinker in his youth, but reformed in the first few years of his marriage and became an active member of the Salvation Army. Isabella coped at home raising her large family. With a new baby arriving every one or two years for almost twenty-one years, this could not have been easy. Alice May was the third girl and sixth child in the family.

George Parkinson was one of eight children born to George (Senior) and Ann Catherine Parkinson, and they, along with several of Alice's uncles and aunts and their children, were still living nearby. The senior Parkinsons were active and capable members of the Hampden community and would have provided advice and support for their growing brood of offspring.

Around 1900 Hampden reverted to its Maori name, Tikokino, as there was already a Hampden in the South Island of New Zealand. The town had been settled early, around 1863.[1] By the time the Parkinsons arrived from Lyttelton it already had a general store selling groceries, drapery, farm goods and hardware. The store also functioned as a post office and savings bank, and the settlers must have been delighted when a telephone office was also established there in 1890. All mail was sent and received daily by a coach service to Waipawa, but the small town of only eight streets was still isolated. Hampden was fifty-two long miles south-west from Napier over a jolting road, and even the nearest railway station was thirteen miles away, at Waipawa.

Hampden was a mill settlement surrounded by native bush. Tall totara, kahikatea, matai and maire grew luxuriantly in the area, especially in the foothills to the west of the village. Sawmills surrounded the town, often moving from site to site as the bush was cut down. Bush fires were an ever-present hazard. Big blazes in 1889 and 1891 saw families removing furniture from their wooden houses and all the adults of the town, including the Parkinsons, were on a round-the-clock watch in case the fires started again. Bush fires razed houses, sawmills, piles of timber

Mail coach
at Hampden (Tikokino).

and wooden tramways. The 1891 fire raged around Hampden for twelve days, and the wooden fences around the town's little cemetery were all taken down to keep them from being destroyed. There was another serious fire in 1896, and more in 1898, 1906 and 1908, so all the residents of the town were constantly on the lookout for smoke and flames. When the school bell and mill whistle sounded together everyone knew it meant 'Fire!'

Both in the mill and in the bush the work was dangerous, and serious accidents were frequent. George Henry, Alice's eldest brother, was killed in such an accident in 1902 when he was just 19 years old.

Hampden School started its life as 'a barn-like building minus comfort of any kind', with one room for the pupils and two for the schoolmaster and his family.[2]

By the time Alice first appeared on the school roll, in 1895, the enlarged wooden buildings were in good condition, well lit and well ventilated. The roll was variable as pupils were often away sick, with regular outbreaks of measles, scarlet fever, whooping cough and rheumatic fever. Children were also needed to stay home and help with bush fires or with 'Mum's washing' or 'Dad's dinner', or to care for younger brothers and sisters. Floods or occasional heavy snowfalls also stopped children from attending school, and many pupils made it to school on only one day in three. Alice, however, learned to read and write at Hampden School and stayed there until the sixth standard — an achievement in itself when movement from one class to the next was ordered not by age but by examination, and when big families like hers were so hard-pressed for labour.

Hampden School was a focus of social life for the district, and many millworkers and farming families were involved in the parties, sports, church services, school picnics and fundraising concerts that were held on school grounds. One of Alice's young unmarried uncles, Arthur Parkinson, gave a series of lectures in the schoolroom on topics such as *The Honey Bee* and *Is Marriage a Failure*?

In the Boer War, when the news of the relief of Mafeking came through, school children paraded through the streets of Hampden behind a Union Jack, and the whole town turned out in style for the coronation of Edward VII in 1902. A highlight of Alice's schooldays would have been a rare school trip by horse and dray to Waipawa and then on to Napier by train. Each child was given a few pence pocket money to spend, which would have made the outing particularly enjoyable. Occasionally a travelling show would call into the isolated settlement and people would flock in from the district to see it. Race days were another local entertainment for those who could afford time off to watch their favourite horses run.

But the reality of daily life in Hampden was harsh for most people. There were wealthy farmers in the district, but money was tight for most of the struggling settlers. In the hungry years of the 1880s, £5 notes were said to be 'as rare as feathers on a frog'. Medical help if needed might take days to arrive. Adults and children alike died from epidemics of meningitis or diphtheria, and mill accidents, bouts of insanity and suicide also took their toll. Funerals were common. In 1891 Alice's bright and enterprising uncle Arthur Henry Parkinson, bee-keeper and occasional lecturer, inexplicably took an overdose of poison and died when he was only 22 years old. Arthur was the Hampden correspondent for the *Waipawa Mail* and also the proprietor of his own Ready Money Store in Hampden, and hence very much involved with the local community. His slow and painful death after three days of suffering would have cast a cloud of misery over the entire district and would have been especially hard for his own grieving family to bear.

In the earliest days, religious gatherings were held in the Hampden schoolroom, with clergymen visiting from Waipawa and Waipukurau to take services. By 1895 the Salvation Army was holding two meetings a month in Hampden and the Parkinsons were regular attenders. George, Isabella and one of Alice's sisters became uniformed officers in the Salvation Army Corps. Sunday school was also held in the schoolroom from 1895, and Alice, along with most of her classmates, enrolled as a pupil. She went on to teach Sunday school herself and to become, at least for a few years, a member of the Salvation Army.

The small town of Hampden was growing steadily, and its residents were proud to now have a bootmaker, bakery, blacksmith's forge, butchery, post office and general store, and even a photographer — all signs of progress and 'getting on'.

Alice left school at fourteen, to go into domestic service in Hastings. Her leaving home meant one less mouth for the family to feed and she may also have sent some of her small wage home to Tikokino to help out with the younger children. Domestic service in those days meant long and often lonely drudgery for young women like Alice. A girl in service was at the mercy of her employers and was required to work from dawn till evening cleaning the house, scouring pots, laying fires and caring for children, with little pay. However, around 1904, when Alice would have left school, there was little other work available for young working-class girls, even those educated to the sixth standard as Alice was.

Not much is known about her years in Hastings, although Edith Amy Todd, who knew her at this period, later testified in a letter that Alice was then '...a bright and cheerful girl, a Christian' who 'loved to be at all the meetings and also to take part, either by praying, speaking, or singing a solo.' When she left home to work at just fourteen she might well have been placed, for her own protection, with another Salvation Army family. Certainly at this period of her life she was a regular churchgoer. She was also 'a welcome visitor', 'steady, modest and respectable'.[3] In Hastings then, Alice Parkinson seemed to have been a well-liked and hard-working young woman. How did she get from this happy state to a charge of murder?

TWO

Napier

Around 1910, after several years of domestic service, Alice left Hastings and found work as a pantrymaid/waitress, first at the Masonic, later at the Central Hotel and then the Albion in Napier. Napier was a busy port town, much livelier than the smaller, newer inland town of Hastings. In Napier, although Alice's was no doubt a live-in position, her social circle widened. Here she met Bert West and started 'walking out' with him.

Walter Albert West worked as a lifter in the Napier railway workshop, helping to maintain passenger cars and railway wagons. A lifter's job was to jack up the heavy wagons to allow work to be performed underneath. They would also help the skilled fitters and boilermakers when needed. Labourers worked for lifters; when Bert West left school, he would have started as a labourer and progressed to being a lifter or leading hand.

The Masonic, before the 1931 Napier earthquake.

Walter Albert West

Bert's parents, Mary Ann and Walter, owned a house in Nelson Crescent, Napier, but had moved out to Taradale in the last few years, six miles from the town centre. Like many other young single men of his day Bert lived with some of his mates in a boarding house in town. Born on 30 November 1894, he was four years younger than Alice. The couple undoubtedly met at the Masonic or one of the other hotels in Napier. Although Alice's Salvation Army upbringing may have given her qualms about overindulgence in drinking, Bert and his friends drank there together regularly.

It seems that Alice always viewed their developing relationship as one that would lead to marriage. She had been away from home working since she was a teenager, and was more than ready to settle down in her own home with a husband and family. But the pool of available men was steadily shrinking. New Zealand had entered the world war along with Britain in August 1914, when war with Germany was declared. Already more and more single men were arriving at army recruiting centres to sign up and were farewelled at proud and tearful functions in town and country halls throughout the district, before going off to training camps in New Zealand or overseas. Three of Alice's brothers, Alfred, Herbert and Ernest, saw active service abroad. Bert West and his fellow railway workers, however, were involved in an essential industry, so they were exempted from military service.

Alice was keen to marry, but Bert, as a young single man, had other plans. However, when in early 1914 Alice became pregnant with his child, he did, both verbally and in writing, promise to marry her and pay the medical expenses for the birth of the coming child. Bert's mother had other ideas. When Alice came to see her to tell her about the baby, she made it clear that this was unwelcome news. Mrs West told Alice that she wanted nothing to do with the whole affair. 'If my son got you into trouble, he must get you out.' Alice had further anxieties. She begged Mary Ann West: 'I want you to get Bert to save his money. He was always in town with [his friend] Cosgrove, drinking.' The other woman was not impressed. She refused her consent for the marriage. '... The boy is under age. He is only twenty, and as long as I have control of him he shall not marry you!' [1]

Bert was due to turn 21 in November 1914, and although they knew that any proposed wedding had to be delayed until then, the young couple still planned to marry. Alice left her hotel job as she could no longer stay at work once her pregnancy began to show. By her own efforts she had managed to save £100, a considerable amount for a working class girl in a variety of low-paid jobs. With Bert's encouragement she withdrew all of the savings from her Post Office Savings Bank account and with this money rented a house in Dalton Street, Napier, furnishing it for a life with Bert and the expected child. Then she moved in to await the birth. She was looking forward to the coming baby. She had been promised the security of marriage, and she would have enjoyed outfitting the home she and Bert were planning to share. However, this was the last period of contentment she was to have for many years.

At the very close of 1914, that first year of the Great War, Alice was suffering her own private torment. She was admitted to Nurse Wilson's home (a small private nursing home) in Napier Crescent on Hospital Hill to have her baby, but the baby was in a transverse position, lying across her in such a way that the birth could never progress. In an era when childbirth was often dangerous for both mother and child, and available pain relief was limited, her labour was prolonged and harrowing. Alice later said that she nearly died. There was no way at that time that both she and her baby could have come out of her labour alive, and on the first day of January 1915 the baby was born dead.

For Alice it was an appalling start to the new year that she had so looked forward to. Grieving, physically knocked around by the birth trauma and almost certainly suffering from what was then called 'puerperal insanity', Alice discharged herself from Nurse Wilson's home. It was far too soon, according to her doctors, who felt she should have stayed there longer. To recuperate she moved into the house of a friend and associate, Mrs Margaret Innes, in Latham Street, Napier. Margaret Innes later testified in court that Alice and Bert had often visited her there in the past. Bert called on the secretary of the Napier Cemetery Trust and applied for a warrant for the interment of a stillborn child. In court, later, the cemetery secretary reported saying, 'I see you have got this girl into trouble. I hope you'll do the right thing by her.' West replied, 'Yes, I am going to marry her,' and the secretary replied 'I'm glad to hear it.'[2]

By now Alice was desperate to marry. In society's eyes she had 'fallen': by giving birth to an illegitimate child she had stained her character. She was no longer an untouched 'would-be' bride, but rather 'used goods'. No matter how discreet she had been she knew that the townsfolk of Napier would inevitably get to know what she had done and would gossip about it. It seemed she had not even told her family at home in Tikokino about her pregnancy and about the sad end of her baby. Now they would surely find out.

Bert too had kept his mouth shut about the coming baby. Each of his close friends and workmates John Forde[3] and Michael Flynn would later testify that Bert had not told them about the impending child or about his marriage plans. Furthermore, it seemed that now there was no longer any baby to worry about, Bert was gradually coming to realise that he was 'off the hook' of marriage and free therefore to carry on with his carefree single life as if nothing had happened.

Alice was still determined to marry Bert, and so began what must have been a long and

John Forde

humiliating campaign. Soon after the appalling stillbirth she called on Canon Laurence Tuke of St Augustine's Church in Napier to ask if he would 'perform a marriage between her and some [unnamed] man.'[4] He told her that if she came at a certain hour he could perform it, but later said in court that a telephone call came to say the marriage was put off. Alice called again the next Saturday and said to Canon Tuke that she wanted to be married to Bert West, and wanted to know if he could perform the marriage ceremony that afternoon. Accordingly, he arranged for the couple to come in to be married at one o'clock that day. He also told Alice that she would need to get the necessary marriage papers from the Government Registrar in Napier and have them properly signed and witnessed before she and Bert could be legally married.

Tuke waited for them in vain at one o'clock; Alice and Bert did not appear. About a week later Alice returned, in company with Margaret Innes, to ask if Bert had been in to give him the marriage papers as he had promised her he would. She would have been dismayed to hear that Bert had been nowhere near Canon Tuke. He told her that he 'thought she had had a fortunate escape from a man who did not meet his appointment with her' but also observed that she was obviously very fond of West. Sadly, Alice told Canon Tuke that she would still marry West 'if he would only come'. Over the eight weeks from the stillbirth, Alice was getting more and more anxious to marry, whilst Bert was getting more and more reluctant.

Alice herself eventually took the initiative and called in to see William Buchanan, Registrar of Births, Deaths and Marriages in Napier to apply for, receive and pay for a marriage certificate, a memorandum of the parties to be married and a marriage licence for her and Bert. These three items she passed on to Bert to deliver to Canon Tuke, as requested by him. Bert never made it to see Canon Tuke, and the marriage papers Alice had applied for were found in the hands of Bert's brother-in-law by the time of her court case and trial.

Throughout this period Bert seemed to have been unable to say no to Alice, or at least to say no directly to her face. She had borne his child and the couple had obviously been close. However, there was something of a mother/child quality to their relationship, as we can see in Alice's letters to him, later produced at her trial:

> Dear Bert,
> Did you go to the registry and fix things up, you might have called in to let me know if you did. So please give Jack an answer as to what I am to do and what time I am to be ready tomorrow. I wish that you were coming up tonight I feel so miserable. Well I hope you have a good time tonight dear & wish you 'Many Happy returns of the day.' Now dear I hope that you prove yourself a man and keep to your promise.
> Your ever loving Alice …

Bert's answer in response, written on the back of Alice's note said:

> Dear Alice Fixed things up. See you 12 20 to morrow afternoon.
> Bert.

Significantly, he added at the bottom of the note the words 'quite sober'.[5] As time went on Alice would have seemed to Bert less like a carefree lover and more like a restricting 'mother figure' who reminded him of his responsibilities and urged him to save money for herself and the coming child. Alice disapproved of heavy drinking. She was described by one of her former employers, Frank Moeller, as being 'fairly strict'.[6] She had seen at first-hand the dire consequences that can come from too much alcohol and too little money.

Repeatedly, although promising Alice he would be there, Bert failed to keep the appointments she made for them to be married. He would explain to her afterwards that he could not get ready in time, or would simply fail to turn up. Nevertheless, to her face he was still promising marriage and a family, while to his friends he was insisting that he wanted nothing to do with either. Bert was having to choose between the thrifty 'tied down' respectable life of a man with a wife and family or the free-wheeling, gambling and drinking culture of life with his mates. After the first of January, when there was no longer any baby to consider, the single life was becoming increasingly attractive. It was Bert's tragedy and Alice's that he did not or could not make this clear to her.

Alice blamed Bert's mother for his growing coolness towards her and felt that Mary Ann West was putting pressure on her son to leave her. In one of her angry (unposted) letters to Mrs West, dated 26 January (1915), Alice expressed her helpless fury:

> Mrs West,
> It doesn't do for people to interfere with any couple going together, so seeing that you have done your utmost to part Bert and I, well, let me tell you, you will be sorry because he shall never marry anybody else ...

and later:

> He turns around and asks me for my last penny — the rotten cur — and still says he is going to marry me ... He came up to me almost every night that I was in the hospital, and I was almost on my dying bed, and he told me to hurry up and get well, and come home, that he was going to marry me. Do you think yourself that he has any principle, although he is your son?

It was significant that these letters to Mrs West were never posted, but in Alice's mind there was obviously warfare between the two of them. All of her resentful hurt and humiliation at the way she had been treated comes out in:

> ... Your son, Bert, is nothing but a low, dirty crawler, and you are worse to interfere; but don't you think that you will have the laugh over me. Bert hasn't been man enough to tell me that he didn't want to marry me. He has been telling me that he is, and that he is supposed to tomorrow morning.

Ominously, she added: 'If he doesn't [turn up to marry me], he will suffer ... '[7] By now, it seemed, Alice was beginning to realise the unthinkable — that Bert would betray her, and that he was making up his mind to leave her.

Obviously the relationship between Alice and Bert was strained and encounters were awkward and uncomfortable, with recriminations on both sides. Increasingly Bert was trying to avoid seeing Alice. When she waited for him after work outside the railway workshops he would turn and go another way home. Alice kept on trying. She was determined to have it out with Bert, and even walked into the railway workshops during working hours trying to see him there, but Bert dodged her whenever he saw her coming. His friends all knew that he wanted to get rid of her, and they helped him to escape. It was a distressing stalemate. Alice had trusted Bert and now he was rejecting her.

She had other problems too. She had not worked for several months and had no source of income. Her nest-egg of £100 was almost gone and she had no choice but to give up her house and stay on as a boarder with Margaret Innes. Alice needed to find money to live on and called back to Canon Tuke, who had treated her kindly in the past, to ask if he knew of any work she could do. He promised to help if he could, but had nothing to offer in the meantime. She sold half of her specially bought furniture and stored the rest at Mrs Innes's house.

Alice was reaching rock bottom. Physically and mentally drained and still grieving for her lost child, she sat at Mrs Innes's house and brooded over Bert's rejection. He had played her false, he had shamelessly used her and led her on to sleep with him and to have his child and now, when she needed him most, he wanted nothing more to do with her. It was an old story — one of the oldest in the book — but it was achingly real to Alice. She had sullied her character. Who would have her now? She was angry with Bert and with herself. Thoughts were hammering away in her brain. Bert, his mother, her mother … what could she do … how could she live … what would she do now?

THREE

Confrontation

Things came to a head on a Sunday night a few weeks later, when two of Bert's friends waylaid Alice in the street and assaulted her, so that she came home with a lump on her lip and a mark on her leg where she had been kicked.[1] It was likely that Alice had been making some wild threats to Bert and he had enlisted his friends to warn her off. By now he was unable to cope face to face with her anger and seems to have been half afraid of her.

Alice was not able to get close enough to Bert to speak to him in private, so she wrote to him. This is from a letter dated Friday night:

> ... Dear Bert, — What in the d------- is the meaning of this foolery? Why didn't you come round to-night when you promised?
> By the holy living smoke I will make you suffer for this ...
> ... You be up here tomorrow night [Saturday] or God help you I will hunt you till I find you and by God you know it ...
> ... You don't deserve to live, you rotter ... Do you think that you can just come when you like. I'll show you different to that ... [2]

Bert was right to be afraid. In a letter written at this time to Isabella Parkinson, her own mother in Tikokino, Alice says:

> ... I won't let him live to ruin another girl, and after treating me like this, well, he is not fit to live. He has always got two coward friends each side of him, afraid to speak to me alone ...

and later in the same letter:

> I will have my revenge, if it is years to come. If he had been a man and acted fair to me, I wouldn't have taken any notice of it. He could easy have told me that he didn't want to marry me, and there would not have been any more said, but now he will suffer as I have. God only knows that I went through enough for him ... [3]

In this wild series of letters that were produced in court at her trial Alice was constantly rehearsing and explaining her grievances. She was angry at Mrs West for interfering in her relationship with Bert, and furious with Bert for deceiving and rejecting her. She described Bert as 'a dirty sneak' and 'a cur' and hotly told Mrs West 'I come from just as good a family as your rotten son Bert does.'

To her own mother Alice wrote to ask for her forgiveness, signing the letter 'Your Broken-hearted Daughter. Alice' she wrote in a postscript: '... It is hard to say good-bye, Mother, but I can't stand it. My heart is breaking.'

She had reached a decision. She would no longer be a helpless victim. Bert had wrecked her life, and so she would wreck his, and they would both die together.

Now that Alice had made up her mind, she was resolute. She felt, as the wronged woman in the case, she had right on her side, and she hit on a way to get herself out of her despair. On March 1 Alice boarded a train to Hastings, just a few miles away from Napier. It was a town she knew well from her years in domestic service. In Hastings she called in to Henry Williams & Sons, Ironmongers, and paid fifteen shillings for a cheap seven-chambered revolver. She also paid out another shilling to buy a box of fifty cartridges.[4] The weapon was small, the kind a woman might tuck into her handbag for self-protection. She gave a false name to the shop assistant, Vernon Taylor, and told him she was taking the gun and ammunition to friends in the country. Taylor knew her by sight if not by name and did not sense anything unusual. He wrapped the gun in brown paper and she put the parcel in her bag and took the train back to Napier. When she felt the weight of the weapon on her lap, she was now committed and would carry out her plan. She went back to Mrs Innes's house to wait for the evening.

Mary Ann West still owned the old house in Nelson Crescent. It was now rented out to Frederick Ashton, a cabinetmaker, and once a month it was Bert's job to call and collect the rent for his mother. Alice knew this, and thought it would be a chance to see Bert alone. In the early evening she called on Ashton and asked if Bert had been round yet for the rent. Ashton told her that Bert would be there about 6:30 pm and because it was a cold night he asked her in to his dining room to wait. Alice stayed there till around 7:30, but Bert did not come that night. It was almost like a repetition of his failure to keep appointments, although this time he did not know that Alice was waiting for him.

Alice was distraught but still resolute. She would keep to her plan. On the next night, 2 March, she went back to see Frederick Ashton and asked the same question: 'Has Bert come for the rent yet?' Ashton told her that Bert had not been and kindly asked her in again to wait for him. He arrived a little later on and Ashton paid the rent. Then Alice went out the back door of the house and she and Bert walked away together. In court Ashton reported later: 'By their talk it seemed as if there had been a bit of a row about something. Could not hear what was said but they were talking in a very sharp manner.'[5] If Alice had any hopeful thoughts of a last-minute reconciliation, it was not going to happen.

John Forde, Bert's workmate and fellow boarder at Michael Flynn's boarding house, had accompanied Bert that night, but when Bert called at Ashton's to collect the rent Forde stopped at a house two doors down to speak to his brother, who was out on the verandah. Soon after this he saw Bert and Alice standing outside the gate. Bert, anxious to get away, said to him, 'Come on John, are you coming home?'[6] John Forde started to walk back towards the centre of town, with Alice and Bert a few yards behind him. Alice had her arm around Bert. Forde said warningly over his shoulder, 'Come on Bert, you had better come away from her.' But Alice was the one to reply. Forde was one of the young men who had waylaid her in the street the previous Sunday. Angrily she stepped forward, punched him on his right ear, and said, 'It's none of your bloody business!' Forde shoved her away roughly and pushed her to the ground. Alice got shakily to her feet and the pair kept on walking. Forde again told Bert to come away from Alice and then, perhaps realising that in knocking Alice down he had gone too far, walked ahead on his own. There was an empty section on the corner of Nelson Crescent and Latham Street. It had willows on each side but there was also a pathway, and Forde used this as a shortcut. By the time he had crossed the section Alice and Bert were just entering it. He heard a shot and turned around to see Bert West drop to the ground.

Now she had started, Alice could not stop. She stood over Bert, firing more shots into his body. Forde could see the pair clearly just a short distance away. Alice, still holding the revolver, looked dangerous. He ran to Flynn's boarding house on nearby Wellesley Road and came back with Flynn. By the time they returned, Bert was lying on the ground groaning, and Alice was close by, slumped up against a tree. She had turned the gun on herself and shot herself in the right temple. Her eyes were glazed and she was barely conscious. A tram conductor, Sydney Otton, who had heard the shots, came to the scene to find Alice leaning against a tree with her arms folded. She was wearing a raincoat that partially hid something in her hands. Otton saw the revolver in her right hand and said 'You better give me that, lady,' and took it from her. Margaret Innes appeared from Latham Street and cried, *'Alice, what have you done!'*

Alice was no longer able to answer. A small crowd was gathering and looking on. Bert, unconscious and bleeding, was removed by the police to Napier Hospital. Otton, Cosgrove and another bystander each took hold of one of Alice's arms and half-walked, half-carried her to Mrs Innes's house close by. From here she was also taken to hospital. For several weeks she would remain there with the bullet still lodged in her head. She was unable to speak for some days and too ill to be questioned by police or to be present at any trial.

But Bert's injuries were more severe. Alice's revolver might have been small and cheap but it was still deadly. He was admitted to hospital in a state of collapse and it was doubtful he ever fully regained consciousness. Alice had shot him in the right temple, on the right side of the neck, in the left cheek and over the left breast. One of the bullets had passed upwards and backwards to the base of the skull, and fragments of bone were found driven into the brain for a considerable distance. There was a large quantity of blood in the left chest cavity. Two of the spent bullets were never located.

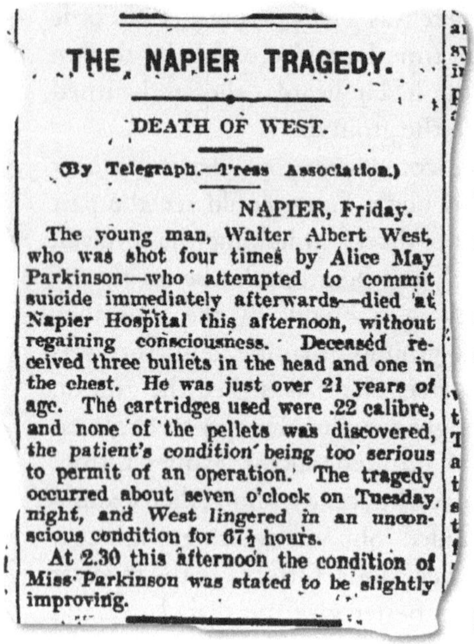
THE NAPIER TRAGEDY.

DEATH OF WEST.

(By Telegraph.—Press Association.)

NAPIER, Friday.

The young man, Walter Albert West, who was shot four times by Alice May Parkinson—who attempted to commit suicide immediately afterwards—died at Napier Hospital this afternoon, without regaining consciousness. Deceased received three bullets in the head and one in the chest. He was just over 21 years of age. The cartridges used were .22 calibre, and none of the pellets was discovered, the patient's condition being too serious to permit of an operation. The tragedy occurred about seven o'clock on Tuesday night, and West lingered in an unconscious condition for 67½ hours.

At 2.30 this afternoon the condition of Miss Parkinson was stated to be slightly improving.

Auckland Star, 6 March 1915

Bert lingered on in pain for three days, drifting in and out of consciousness before dying in the afternoon of 5 March. Although he had multiple injuries, the eventual cause of death was given by his doctors as laceration of the brain by the passage of a bullet. To satisfy police procedures, his body was identified in the morgue by his father, Walter West, who recognised him by his toes. His big toe and second toe were joined together. [7]

Sometimes official records tell a poignant story. Among the fragile files of the New Zealand National Archives is a set entitled 'Intention of Marriage Within Three Calendar Months'. On 13 February 1915 there is an entry for Alice Parkinson — Waitress

25 (years) and for Bert West — Railway Lifter 21 (years). Alice has willingly signed — her signature is there — but Bert's is not. Underneath the two entries is a comment from Canon Tuke:

> No marriage was performed. The woman came twice but West did not appear. The sequel was that Parkinson murdered West whom she shot with a revolver.

Four

Aftermath

The coroner's inquest was held in Napier seven weeks later, on 21 April, when Alice was finally well enough to be present. She had made a slow recovery from the gunshot wound and may still have been unable to comprehend much of what was going on. She wore a large black hat and was dressed in a blue skirt and jacket with a white lace collar. Barney Dolan, a Napier lawyer, had been found to represent her. John Forde, his brother George, the Napier police and the hospital doctors all presented their evidence to the coroner. At the end of the hearing the Coroner declared that Bert died on 5 March 'as the result of wounds intentionally inflicted on him by Alice Parkinson by means of a revolver on the evening of the 2nd day of March 1915.'

Alice was then charged with the murder of Walter Albert West and Dolan's request for bail was refused. She was remanded in custody until the next Monday. However, the police reported her doctors' instructions that she continue to be kept under medical observation and she may well have been returned to Napier Hospital rather than to the town gaol at this time.

It was wartime. On 25 April New Zealand troops had landed on the beaches of Gallipoli. Black-bordered lists of casualties were appearing in newspapers and people were starting to ask why so many young men were dying. Despite the great shadow of war, Alice's case was catching the national imagination. She had shot her former lover down in public — almost in the street — in a dramatic confrontation. Furthermore, she had used a gun rather than poison, which was then the more customary 'woman's method'.

On 26 April, in a preliminary hearing in the Napier Magistrate's Court, Alice was formally charged with murder. Canon

Tuke, John Forde, Mary Ann West, Margaret Innes and the police all gave evidence, and Alice's letters were read aloud in court. Constable John Rosanoski had been around to Mrs Innes's house and searched through Alice's belongings. He had found the cartridge box with the remaining 43 of her 50 cartridges bought in Hastings. In a tin trunk he had also found three of her unposted letters. Two of these were addressed to the Sergeant of Police with a request that they be opened and read by him before being forwarded on to Mrs Walter West at Taradale. The third letter was addressed to her mother, Mrs George Parkinson, in Tikokino. It was these letters, with their confused explanations, threats and accusations, and also some of the letters she had written to Bert in the past, that were read aloud in court. Taken together, they were damning. Statements such as: 'I am on my own, but I will have my revenge' and 'I can't stand it any more. I am going to shoot the both of us' had the whole court agog.

In the end the result was inevitable. Alice was asked if she had anything to say and, instructed by Barney Dolan, said in calm tones, 'I reserve my defence.'[1] The Napier magistrate, Samuel Ernest McCarthy, found she had a case to answer and she was committed to stand trial for murder at the next sitting of the Supreme Court in Napier, in June 1915. This one would be a jury trial.

The New Zealand weekly *Truth* had picked up the story and was following it closely. Page 4 of Saturday 1 May had banner headlines:

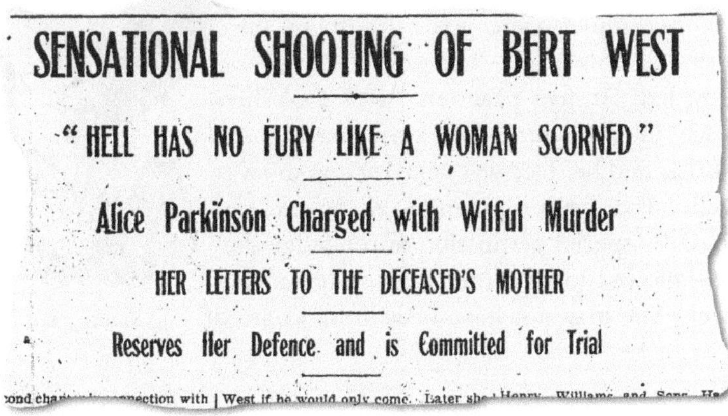

SENSATIONAL SHOOTING OF BERT WEST

"HELL HAS NO FURY LIKE A WOMAN SCORNED"

Alice Parkinson Charged with Wilful Murder

HER LETTERS TO THE DECEASED'S MOTHER

Reserves Her Defence and is Committed for Trial

FIVE

Trial

In the Supreme Court of New Zealand

NAPIER CRIMINAL SITTINGS
9th June 1915

Before His Honour the Chief Justice

Rex v. ALICE MAY PARKINSON
(Murder)

Cornford for the Crown
Dolan for the Accused[1]

Alice's trial for murder duly started on the morning of 9 June. The case was a significant one. Sir Robert Stout, the Chief Justice of New Zealand, was presiding.

Henry Cornford, the Crown Solicitor, appeared for the Crown, and Bernard (Barney) Dolan again represented Alice. In the language of the court, she would from now on be referred to as 'the accused' and Bert had become merely 'the deceased'.

ALICE PARKINSON
NZ Truth, 24 April 1915

A jury of twelve local men was sworn in;[2] no women were permitted to be on juries at this time. The courtroom was crowded. At five past ten Alice took her place in the court. She was wearing dark clothes and her face was veiled. How she was feeling is difficult to imagine, as she gave no sign.[3] By special permission of the judge she was allowed to sit rather than stand in the dock. She may not have been fully aware of it, but the stakes were high. In 1915 New Zealand still had the death penalty in place and if Alice was found guilty she could be hanged. The New Zealand judiciary had already hanged one woman for murder — Minnie Dean, the so-called Winton baby farmer, in 1895.[4]

Yet again, Alice's story was repeated as the events leading up to the shooting were told for the third time. The doctors who had treated Bert in hospital gave evidence, although one of them, Dr John Leahy, was now on his way overseas to serve at the front and his evidence was read by the court registrar. Canon Tuke, the cleric, gave his evidence of appointments made and not kept and of Alice's desperation to marry Bert, although he observed that she did not weep and that he had seen other brides much more perturbed than the accused was.[5] Clearly, in his experience, desertion at the altar was not unknown.

Forde, Otton, Taylor, Mary Ann West and Margaret Innes were all called to give evidence for the Crown (or prosecution). Constable Rosanoski gave his evidence and Alice's letters were produced and read to the court. Detective Sergeant Alfred Ward, who took Alice to the hospital on the night of 2 March, then produced her revolver. He pointed out that the gun had seven chambers and of these seven, five were now empty. Two still held unexploded bullets and 'the seven make up the full complement' of the weapon. Ward told the court that when he found Alice slumped on the ground she was suffering from a wound in the head, although under cross-examination from Barney Dolan he admitted that she had never been charged with attempted suicide. This ended the case for the prosecution. Things did not look good for Alice.

B. J. DOLAN

NZ Truth, 16 December 1916.

Barney Dolan, for the accused, wanted to have evidence of Alice's good character heard in court and also wanted her unstable mental condition at the time of the shooting to be recognised. His best chance of having the charge reduced or dismissed lay with evoking sympathy for Alice as a disturbed and betrayed young woman. He needed to convince the judge and jury that Alice had acted as she did only because her disordered mind had reached some kind of breaking point. In this way he might be able to counteract some of the more damning evidence of her letters.

Dolan called George Parkinson, Alice's father, who had come from Tikokino to give evidence. George and Isabella had always loved and supported Alice and would continue to do so throughout their lives. George told the court that Alice never showed any signs of violent conduct when she lived at home in Tikokino. He also acknowledged that two of Alice's uncles had committed suicide. Perhaps understandably with so many children, George could not recall the year of Alice's birth or the date of her birthday.

John Garrett, her Tikokino Sunday school teacher, testified that he had known her all his life and that she was 'very quiet and orderly. Her parents are respectable people. Her father and mother and one sister are uniformed officers in the Salvation Army.' Afterwards two of Alice's former employers in Napier, the licensees of the Masonic and the Central hotels, gave evidence. Both agreed that her conduct while working for them was very good, and that they had never heard her use abusive language.

Then it was Alice's turn to take the stand, and Barney Dolan led her slowly through her evidence. She told the court about meeting Bert some time in 1913, and that Mrs Innes had introduced them. Once more she went through the agony of the baby's death and Bert's repeated promises of marriage.

> West sent me to Canon Tukes. We were to be married on a Saturday, about a fortnight [before] the tragedy, at one o'clock. That day I went round to Flynn, at 20 past 12. When I saw him he was in his working clothes. I asked him what he was going to do. He wanted me to go to Canon

> Tukes to apologise to the Canon and tell him that he could not get there. I said, No you go yourself and apologise. He took my bike round to see Canon Tukes. He did not go to Canon Tukes.[6]

By the time she got to the shooting the whole court was on edge and the jury members were listening closely.

> I said 'Why are you such a coward to bring your mates out to bully me?' I said 'When are you going to marry me?' He turned round and said 'Marry you! I don't b----- well intend to marry you.' He said, 'Get to Hell out of it. West said, 'Now, will you leave me alone.' He pushed me down. I nearly fell. I said, 'By God, Bert West, if you do not marry me I will go mad.' I said, 'If you do not marry me tomorrow I will shoot you dead at 12 o'clock ... Then I pointed the revolver at him. I was carrying it in my pocket, loaded. I pointed the revolver at his chest.'

This is the final confrontation:

> He tried to snatch the revolver away. He got hold of my hand and pushed it back like this. [indicating] He said, 'By God I will fix you up.' I felt a sharp sting in my right temple. He did not have the revolver in his hand. I did not know any more after till I woke up in the hospital.

Under cross questioning from the Crown Prosecutor, Alice again relived the last few moments of her fatal encounter with Bert.

> We were standing side by side when he snatched my hand. He was on my right side — just half way on. He was facing across me. I felt the sting in the right temple. His left hand held my right hand. I knew nothing after feeling the sting ... I fancy I heard three or four shots. I do not know who fired them. I never lost hold of the revolver ...

Cornford asked a few more questions of Alice, seeking to blacken her character. What was she doing after she left her last job at the Albion Hotel? Who had she been living with? Alice answered his questions truthfully: 'The child was born about two months after I left [my last job]. I lived in my own home. Mrs Innes used to come up, but I slept alone.' More damningly, however, she also told Cornford and the court 'when I wrote the letter [to her mother] I had it in my mind to kill West and myself.'

Dolan then called Alice's Napier doctor, Thomas Johnson, who confirmed that she had an extremely difficult confinement only eight weeks earlier and had discharged herself from hospital too soon. He told the court that after the birth of the child he had met with Bert and the young man had promised to pay the costs of Alice's confinement. Bert had paid about one third when the tragedy occurred. Johnson's testimony closed the evidence for the defence and the trial was finished for the day. The next day, the two lawyers would address the court and the judge would give his summing up. Tomorrow, the jury must make its decision.

On the next day of the trial the courtroom was packed again, with many women sitting in the public gallery. There was a tense silence when Barney Dolan rose to address the jury. Dolan was a convivial character. He was an Irish lawyer, fond of society and conversation and the chief of the Napier Orphans, a social and fund-raising society. Dolan was a good speaker. He began by asking the jurors to put aside any rumours they may have heard outside the evidence given, regarding the conduct of the accused.

> Rumour was a lying jade ... rumour had prompted the Crown solicitor to put the questions as to who had visited the accused at Dalton Street. Was there a tittle of evidence in support of the innuendo? No! The girl was as true to West as the needle was to the Pole.

As always, Dolan aimed to stir the jury to compassion for Alice's situation. Something of the flavour of his address comes out in:

> ... The letters of the accused were not in the language of Belgravia, but it was a country girl corrupted by malign influences in town, the mother of an illegitimate child, the target of Mother Grundy [rumour and gossip] spurned by her paramour, rebuffed by his relations — a country girl pouring out her love and her hate in the agonies of her pregnancy and the tortures of her labour. Provocation! Was there ever as much? She had borne the child of the deceased. She had been thumped down in his presence in the public

Sir Robert Stout KCMG (1844–1930) was Premier of New Zealand on two occasions in the late 19th century, and later Chief Justice of New Zealand. He was the only person to hold both these offices. He was noted for his support of liberal causes such as women's suffrage, and for his strong belief that philosophy and theory should always triumph over political expediency.
PAColl-5800-59, Alexander Turnbull Library

> street — she, who had bought with her scanty savings the very marriage bed on which they were to lie ... [7]

Dolan pointed out to the jury that the charge of murder still had to be proven, and he put forward the suggestion that in grabbing Alice's arm to try to take the revolver away from her it was Bert himself who fired the first fatal shot.

> All the features of the melodrama were the property of the Crown in this case — incriminating letters, the meeting, the corpse and the smoking revolver. But, who fired the first shot? ... Did not the girl's statement suggest the only practicable theory — West's hand over the girl's hand, her hand on the trigger, his fingers grasping it as he says, 'By God I'll fix you!' — his shot! ... 'If West fired the first shot,' he told the jury, 'they could conclude that she fired the fatal shot in self defence.'

Dolan spoke for more than an hour. It was powerful oratory. You can sense the rhythm of his speech and the rise and fall of his voice, even from the words on the page. He suggested to the jury that Alice's medical history would justify an acquittal on the grounds of insanity and that the provocation she had received would absolutely reduce the capital charge. He submitted that the defence was alternative but also that the jury would absolutely justify themselves in returning a verdict of not guilty.

Where Barney Dolan was impassioned Crown Prosecutor Cornford was cool. Throughout his much shorter address he referred to Bert West as a 'boy' and said to the jury that he could not believe that a boy of eighteen could be called the seducer of a woman of twenty-one. He told the jury that Alice's letters were hardly the letters of anyone who was 'deeply in love with a boy' and suggested to them that Bert was frightened of Alice. He asked them to put aside any idea that Alice fired those five shots 'unknowingly' and said to the jury and the crowded court, 'In the face of the accused's letters and the evidence of the prosecution could the jury have the slightest doubt that there was an intention to kill and that that intention was carried out.'[8]

Now Chief Justice Sir Robert Stout began his summing up of the case for the jury. He was not impressed by Dolan's oratory. He outlined the facts of the case and said to the jury:

> Because the deceased had refused to marry her that was no reason why she should have shot him. She could have sued him in the courts. There was no provocation for the act. There was no provocation at all. His voice had now been closed by her and he could not give evidence.[9]

Stout told the jury that the evidence before them did not point to insanity but that they had to determine this. He instructed the jury they must bring in one of three verdicts:

> First: Guilty.
> Second: Guilty but her power of self-control lost, owing to suffering.
> Third: Not Guilty on the grounds of insanity.

They must weigh the evidence carefully and give their verdict accordingly. It was a big responsibility for the twelve men: Alice's life could hang on their decision. At 12:25 pm they retired to consider their verdict. At three o'clock they filed back into the courtroom and the foreman of the jury told the judge that they were unable to agree on a verdict and that there seemed no prospect of agreement. Chief Justice Stout was implacable. He told them they would have to retire again. The jurymen returned to court at 3:35. Together they had reached what they hoped would be a compromise. Their foreman told the judge that they had found the accused guilty of manslaughter, but they had also added a rider to the verdict. They had made a strong recommendation for mercy for the accused on account of the provocation she had received.

Barney Dolan was quick to realise what this verdict might mean for Alice. He pleaded with the judge, asking Stout to 'extend to this woman his accustomed benignity and clemency' and asked that Stout, in sentencing Alice, be as lenient as he possibly could be under the circumstances. Stout remained unmoved. He told the court that in his opinion there was no provocation. It was cold premeditated murder. The jury had obviously taken a clement

Napier's historic prison.

view of the case because the accused was a woman. He told the court that if he were to extend clemency he would be encouraging crime and assassination. If he did that, every woman who found that a man would not marry her would do the same thing. Life would no longer be safe. In the silence that followed this pronouncement, Stout sentenced the prisoner to imprisonment for manslaughter for the term of her natural life.

There was an audible gasp from the crowded courtroom. Alice did not outwardly react, and stepped down from the dock calmly. It was the chivalrous members of her jury who reacted the most markedly to Stout's harsh sentence. A sentence for life at this time meant gaol for the rest of your life, rather than for a set period of years. While Alice was led away from the court, the jurymen gathered in a huddle to discuss what just happened. They were unhappy at the sentence and disturbed at their part in bringing it about. They had hoped that by bringing in a rider asking for mercy, Alice would have been treated more kindly by the judge. In a very unusual act for a jury, they decided to petition the New Zealand government for a remission of Alice's harsh sentence. Together they wrote a letter of petition and all of them signed it.

Barney Dolan too was unhappy at the sentence. He seemed to have genuinely felt that Alice had a rough deal from the judiciary and he would continue to fight for her over the next few years. Almost immediately he announced his decision to appeal the sentence. Dolan acted quickly. Then, as now, a prisoner cannot be retried for the same offence. All Dolan could do was suggest there was something wrong with the conduct of the trial itself. He appealed the sentence on two grounds: that the jury was misdirected in that they were not told beforehand that their recommendation for mercy might not necessarily be followed by the judge; and that there were two police constables and a caterer also in the jury room while the jurymen were deliberating and their presence could have meant there would have to be a newly sworn-in jury and a complete retrial. It was a long shot. Dolan did not have much to go on and knew it, but he was doing his best.

Alice was taken back from the Supreme Court to the old gaol on Napier Hill to await the result of the appeal. She had been there since 21 April. Once more she walked through the heavy wooden doors in the perimeter stone wall. The gaol was a grim, shabby place with a small exercise yard near the cells. In the past, prisoners had been hanged in a corner of this yard and the graves of these unfortunate men were still there at the gaol. Napier was a mixed prison although, as usual, far more men than women were housed there.

Alice did not have much longer to stay there. One week later, in the Supreme Court in Napier on 17 June, Chief Justice Sir Robert Stout heard Dolan's appeal.[10] In effect he was sitting in judgment on his own judgment, which sounds unbelievable today. Predictably, Stout rejected the appeal and Alice's fate was sealed. There would be no escape from her life sentence. She was to be sent away from Napier, down to the South Island, to serve out her time at Addington Prison in Christchurch.

Addington prison, early days.

SIX

Addington

Alice arrived at Addington Prison (later known as Addington Reformatory) around 22 June 1915. Prison files give an indication of her appearance at this time. She was not a big woman — she stood five feet two inches tall, was of medium build and with a fresh complexion. Her hair was dark brown and her eyes blue/grey. She had a small scar on her right temple where the bullet entered her head. She was also quick to anger and easily upset. There were reports in this early part of her sentence of occasional threats to staff or to other inmates. On one occasion she was punished with twenty-four hours on bread and water. She was dazed and unhappy.[1]

Addington had been opened in July 1913 as a prison for women serving sentences of longer than three months. It was not a new building, having been originally built in the early 1860s to ease the overcrowding at Lyttelton Gaol, then the major prison for the Canterbury region. In the 1870s the Christchurch Lock Hospital was also housed at Addington Prison. At this time women suspected of being prostitutes could be detained in a lock hospital and forced to submit to a genital examination and to remain there to undergo treatment if any infection was found. The lock hospitals were hated institutions, and the combined prison cum lock hospital must have been a fearful and forbidding place for women.[2] In 1896 the Christchurch Samaritan Home took over the complex and used it as an institutional home for unmarried mothers and old people for several years, until the Justice Department resumed control of the buildings in 1912. By the time Alice arrived at the prison in 1915 it had already had a long and chequered history and its buildings were run down and dilapidated. Only one of the two large buildings was still fit for use and it was in this building that all the female prisoners, including Alice, were housed.

Addington took all types of female offenders. As a new prisoner, Alice would have been officially received into the prison along with any other newcomers that day, and then classified. Classification was very important in the prison system. Ideally it meant grouping the inmates into 'classes' and housing each class in a separate area with little or no contact with any other class. How Alice was classified would have depended largely on her crime and character and later on her behaviour while in prison. At Addington at this time, however, the classification method was never really successful. In effect, how a woman was classified had more to do with how many times she had been convicted and how much of a problem or how well behaved she was. All groups were housed in the same building, although on different floors. In reality it was impossible to keep hardened old lags and new or young offenders entirely apart from each other, and there were often discipline problems. Alice, exhausted after the trial, and the long journey from Napier and still unwell, would have been hard to classify. She had probably sailed to the Christchurch port of Lyttelton and certainly would have flinched at the public shame of a prison escort. She was a first offender, but one who had been convicted of an extremely serious crime. In addition, she was vulnerable in that she was still dazed from the bullet lodged in her brain and still grieving for her lost infant. Now, so far away from Tikokino and Napier that it was almost impossible for her parents or any friends to visit her, she would have been angry and desolate.

It is hard to know whether she shared a cell with anyone else.[3] Addington in 1915 had forty-five beds available, while the greatest number of prisoners at any one time that year was forty-eight, so there must have been some doubling up. However, the indeterminate length of her sentence meant she was in prison for the long haul, and that, together with her occasional fits of anger, meant that Alice was most likely left on her own. Her cell would have been spartan. Each cell contained:

bedstead or hammock
flock mattress
flock pillow
four blankets (for the cold and damp Christchurch winters)
tin basin
coir cell brush
candlestick
salt cellar
tin jug
tin knife
enamel chamber pot
tin pint (cup or mug)
tin spoon
stool
table
tin plate
slate
hair brush
hair comb
cleaning box
copy of the prison rules
toothbrush.

Clean clothing was issued once a week and, around 1917, all of the women's clothing would have been marked with the broad prison arrow. The clothing allowance for women seems reasonably generous though the prison authorities would have been looking to keep inmates clean and warm rather than catering for individual fit or fashion. The prescribed list for Alice and her fellow prisoners was:

two sacking aprons
one white apron
one bonnet
two pairs of calico drawers (underwear)
two handkerchiefs
two dungaree jackets (made from a coarse Indian calico)
one serge jacket for winter (only in the colder South Island prisons such as Addington)
two coloured neckerchiefs
two flannel petticoats
one linsey petticoat (cloth made from linen and wool)
two cotton shifts
two flannel shifts
one pair of shoes
two dungaree skirts
one pair of stays
two pairs of stockings
two nightdresses
two hand towels and one bath towel

From 1915 all women were also issued with sanitary towels. They were allowed one bath a week and, unlike male prisoners of the time, were not required to cut their hair.

The food at Addington was plain but seems to have been reasonably nourishing. Each day inmates such as Alice received a measured amount of oatmeal, bread, potatoes, sugar, salt and pepper, meat, carrots, turnips, onions and tea. As they worked hard, the women needed to be well nourished. Alice and the other inmates all performed the same labour. Their days were spent largely in cleaning, sewing, washing, ironing and maintaining the prison grounds, although male prisoners from Lyttelton Gaol did some of the heaviest outdoor work. The women at Addington did all their own laundry as well as taking in the washing for the men's prison at Lyttelton. In addition to this they made their own prison clothing, knitted socks and made cardigans for the men's prisons all around the country. They also sewed very heavy kit bags. It was tiring and monotonous work, designed to punish the women and to deter them from re-offending, rather than reform them. It was believed by the authorities that 'female reformation' was beyond the great majority of women offenders. Throughout the rest of the Great War, Alice and her fellow prisoners also did a lot of knitting and sewing for patriotic groups to send to soldiers at the front. Most of this work was done by hand because, although the prison did have a couple of sewing machines, Matron Madeline McBryde felt that the women would be incapable of using the machines.

At Addington, the women were kept busy and under control by the more or less industrial nature of the work they did. Education programmes were minimal. From 1916 a former teacher from the Christchurch Technical College came to the prison to give lessons and demonstrations of 'domestic economy'. Also, from 1919 the Justice Department allowed the women to attend classes at the prison in writing, reading and cooking — although these classes were short-lived and were stopped altogether in 1921. It was hard to evaluate how much benefit these brief education programmes were for Alice and the other imprisoned women, but at least they broke the monotony of constant cleaning, sewing, washing and ironing.

It was a world largely without men. Once a week the Lyttelton Gaoler visited Addington to supervise the work there, and a male officer controlled the entrance gate, but the rest of the prison was under female control. Women such as Matron McBryde managed the prison on a daily basis, writing reports on inmates, ordering supplies and controlling junior prison officers. Their work was not easy. Overcrowding of cells and often difficult inmates mixing closely together could result in an explosive situation. There were complaints about the behaviour at Addington and about young runaway escapees from the prison roaming the streets of Christchurch and getting into trouble. The creaky old buildings on the site did not make things any easier. Alterations and improvements to the prison buildings came very slowly. The oldest of the two on the Addington site was found to have dry rot and was eventually demolished. Bathing and laundry facilities at the prison were not improved until two years into Alice's stay there.

By 1919 Addington Reformatory had a refractory (punishment) cell for badly behaved inmates and a padded cell for 'fractious cases', but reports of the time said that this particular cell was only occasionally put to use. Upstairs in the building was a small church or chapel, and staff and inmates had a break from the drudgery of the working week by attending the Sunday church services held there. Alice played the organ for some of these. With her Salvation Army childhood, the familiar Bible stories and hymns must have provided some times of quiet reflection for her; she would have needed these occasional moments of peace. When she first arrived at Addington in June 1915, her future stretched out before her as a young woman condemned to a confined life in a small cell. From this time onwards she would be watched and controlled day and night by warders. She had been denied the husband she had always expected to have and the children she wanted so badly. Understandably, in the first years of her sentence at Addington, Alice was restless and deeply unhappy. Like her fellow prisoners she was permitted to write a letter of only one page just once every three months, and few visitors came to see her. It must have seemed to her, after all the public uproar of her trial and sentencing, that she was cut off from the world outside the prison and that the outside world had forgotten her.

Addington prison.

Inside Addington prison: today it is a backpacker hostel.

SEVEN

Protest

But Alice had not been forgotten. Almost immediately after her trial and Barney Dolan's appeal, groups and individuals began to protest at the severity of her sentence. The New Zealand weekly paper *Truth* was one of the earliest. Its issue of 26 June 1915 had the headline:

POOR ALICE PARKINSON

No "Unwritten Law" in God's Own

"Truth" does not want to rub it into His Honor Sir Robert Stout too

The article that followed was to be the first of many in the long fight for Alice Parkinson's freedom. It was a call to arms:

> *Truth* does not want to rub it into His Honor Sir Robert Stout too hard, but it cannot leave the consideration of the subject of punishment for crime without referring to the almost brutal sentence passed by the Chief Justice on the woman, Alice Parkinson, at Napier, for the shooting of Walter Albert West.

The article went on to ponder the ageing Sir Robert Stout's administration of justice:

> Of late, however, something untoward seems to have occurred which has soured the milk of human kindness in

> him; or old age is impairing his judicial sense of proportion? Only on one or other of these grounds can *Truth* understand the callous sentence he inflicted upon poor Alice Parkinson despite the jury's strong recommendation to mercy. It is safe to say that in no other part of the British Empire could such a vicious sentence follow upon such a sympathetic verdict.

In *Truth*'s opinion, 'the unfortunate female had been as much sinned against as she had sinned.' The article ended by urging every man and woman in New Zealand possessed of any 'humanitarian feelings or sense of justice' to petition the Ministry of Justice and Cabinet and to organise protest meetings on Alice's behalf in 'every town in the Dominion'.

The tone of the article was urgent. 'Let those who see eye to eye with *Truth* in these matters act promptly, for the time is short. This paper will do all it can to further the success of any movement ... Do it now!'[1] It was becoming clear that very many newspaper readers from up and down the country were heeding this call from *Truth*. Although more punitive members of the public would always see Alice as a girl 'no better than she ought to be' who got what she deserved, Alice's plight did seem to resonate with many people who saw her instead as a young woman who had been most grievously wronged. Spurned and betrayed by her seducer Bert West and callously struck down in the street by his friends, she was viewed as a working-class woman who was now in gaol without friends and without hope. As such, she was a figure to be pitied and one that many groups and individuals wanted to help. Every day now, more and more young men were dying on overseas battlefields and New Zealanders at home could do nothing to save them. Alice Parkinson was someone who was here, close at hand someone they could start to put their energies into saving, and they did.

Truth's headline for 10 July read:

ALICE PARKINSON'S POSITION

An Appeal for Clemency to the Imprisoned Woman

PETITIONS FREELY SIGNED PRAYING FOR HER RELEASE

To be Forwarded to the Governor-in-Council

The Voice of the People Demand Justice for Her

The article claimed proudly that *Truth*'s appeal for Alice Parkinson had met with a most sympathetic response from all over New Zealand. Requests for petition forms came in from many districts, and women's societies and other organisations were arranging to call public meetings to protest at Judge Robert Stout's ignoring of the jury's recommendation of mercy. Letters of sympathy for Alice and protests at the harshness of her sentence had been arriving at *Truth*'s head office — too many for the newspaper to publish, although it could not resist providing extracts from some of the more 'pithy' ones.

> Alice Parkinson — who was she? Only a common tea-room waitress, that had made herself too cheap to one of the boys, who had since failed to 'make good', — an everyday occurrence ... Besides, she was poor. Her people were unknown and of no account. Therefore there was no kudos for the plute [i.e. plutocratic or rich] pen-pushers in championing her case against the all-powerful Justice Department ... That the judge practically ignored the jury's finding ... that his Honour, the Chief Justice, Sir Robert Stout, constituted himself Judge and jury in one, did not trouble them.[2]

Truth went on to tell its readers that an anonymous correspondent had sent in eight shillings to help pay the expenses of the appeal for Alice, but the paper also said that it had not opened any subscription list for this purpose and that the cost of printing petitions and placards would be borne by itself alone. Clearly *Truth* was in it for the long haul.

Truth's printed petition form was to be a significant factor in the fight for Alice's freedom. It was from the 'under-signed electors in the Dominion of New Zealand' and was addressed to His Excellency the Governor in Council. The petition had been carefully drawn up. Its text set out Alice's killing of Bert and her trial and sentence, but, following this, also clearly set out some of the extenuating circumstances for her behaviour — her difficult labour and dead baby, Bert West's desertion and the loss of her savings all spent on account of Bert's false promise to marry. The petition also mentioned Alice's youth and her good character prior to her offence. The petitioners asked for mercy for Alice on these grounds and prayed that the sentence imposed on her might be reduced. Underneath this form were spaces for the supporters to sign their names. *Truth* printed a large number of these petition forms and held them at its office in Luke's Lane in Wellington and also at its Auckland and Christchurch offices. The newspaper invited anyone interested to call in and collect these forms or to apply for them in writing, and many people did.[3]

The New Zealand labour movement also took up Alice's case in the cause of women's rights. The Social Democratic Party and the United Federation of Labour had each held annual conferences in July 1915 and Alice's offence and trial, still featuring in the newspapers, had been discussed at each one.[4]

The members of the Social Democratic Party did not waste any time. Its Wellington and Petone branches formed a joint steering committee comprising three men and also three from the women's section of the party.[5] They organised a mass meeting to be held at the recently built People's Picture Palace, at 17 Manners Street in downtown Wellington. One of the members of this committee was Harry Holland, editor of the influential United Federation of Labour weekly newspaper, the *Maoriland Worker.* Trade unionist, a socialist and a journalist, Holland, was a champion of the worker, the powerless and the deprived. He was also an eloquent writer and speaker. Alice Parkinson was a penniless working-class woman who had 'fallen' and was in need of help. Members of the labour movement of New Zealand were more than willing to support her. She was one of their own.

Holland himself spoke to the crowded audience. People had swarmed into the People's Picture Palace to hear him deliver a long and passionate speech, and at its end he was repeatedly applauded. Holland then used the pages of the *Maoriland Worker* to support Alice's cause. His ringing article of 28 July 1915 entitled, in big black letters, 'A Plea for Alice Parkinson' was an account of his Picture Palace speech the previous Sunday night. In this article Holland used Alice's case to look at the far bigger picture — the double standard of the day and the plight of women who must bear the stigma of illegitimate pregnancy and take the blame and the consequences for this:

> ... No one would be foolish enough to say that the woman is not often as much to blame as the man. But what must not be lost sight of is the fact that it is always the woman who pays — who bears the full weight of the burden of shame and suffering that a mock-moral — or, rather, immoral — Society imposes for the 'sin' of parenthood under unorthodox circumstances. This is so because woman is economically unfree. The man in the case may be a moral leper; his reputation may reek of the sewer; but Society (more especially if he be wealthy) will fling its doors wide open to him.

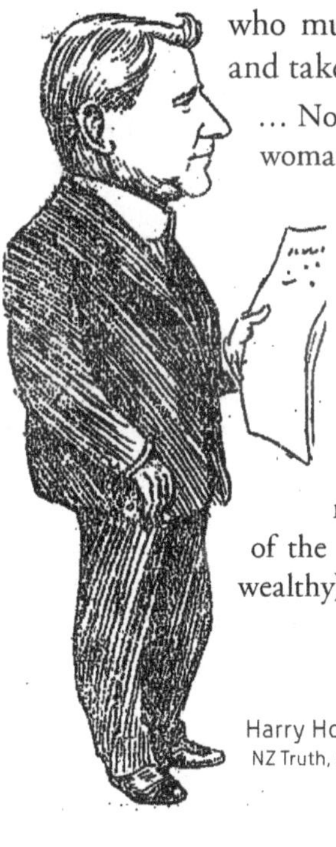

Harry Holland.
NZ Truth, 6 July 1918

Holland went on to arouse the sympathy of his readers for the

> basely-deserted girl whose heart broke and whose mind failed in that desolated Gethsemane. In the hour of her overwhelming despair she hurled her betrayer to a swift grave! It is certainly a dreadful deed, an act not to be encouraged. BUT WAS SHE RESPONSIBLE? Society provided no adequate punishment for the man. Society flung the woman among hissing serpents and slow-burning fires. Surely whatever crime there was belongs not to the girl, but to Society.

As the *Truth* editorial had done, Harry Holland attacked the formidable Chief Justice Sir Robert Stout:

> ... Because the judge refused to take notice of the jury, because the judge was unable or unwilling to understand the driving force that the psychology of human despair operates in such an hour of bloody sweat and agony — because of this Alice Parkinson is hurled to a living death. All the horrors and brutalities of a prison experience are to be hers FOR THE TERM OF HER NATURAL LIFE![6]

Along with *Truth*, Holland and the *Maoriland Worker* would continue the fight for Alice over the next few years. Indeed

PETITION

To His Royal Highness the Prince of Wales

PRAYING FOR THE RELEASE FROM PRISON OF ALICE PARKINSON, NOW SERVING A LIFE SENTENCE.

Under great provocation, this unfortunate woman shot a man who, under the promise of marriage, seduced and betrayed her.

And your petitioners ever humbly pray.

NAME	ADDRESS	NAME	ADDRESS

Holland and his fellow supporters from the Social Democratic Party and the United Federation of Labour would go even further than *Truth*. Whereas *Truth* was planning to petition the Crown to ask for clemency for Alice and a reduction in her sentence, the *Maoriland Worker* was demanding nothing less than her release from gaol. Followers of the New Zealand labour movement must direct their efforts to '… swing outward her prison doors … '[7] It was a bold stance they were taking and not one that would endear the newspaper to Chief Justice Stout or to many of the more judgmental members of New Zealand society.

Page three of the *Maoriland Worker* of 28 July 1915 featured a large photograph of Alice (above). She has an oval face and a cloud of dark hair. She stares out of the picture unsmiling but calm, although perhaps slightly apprehensive. She is nicely dressed, with a small frill of lace at the cuffs of her sleeves. Her hands hold a partially open book, but she does not seem to be studying it, so that the book may be just a photographer's prop. She is leaning

Alice Parkinson Release Fund

	£	s.	d.
Received at "The Worker" office:			
Previously acknowledged ...	0	5	0
L.K.N.	0	5	0
Collected at S.D.P. Meeting	3	17	2
Collected by Mrs. Bradley (St. Albans)	0	9	6
Received by Mrs. Rae:			
Mr. Sullivan	0	2	6
Mrs. Bayley	0	2	6
Lady (Cuba Street)	0	1	0
Sympathiser	0	0	6
F. Johnson	0	2	0

CER is Clara Ann Rae.

Wanted Funds

TO SECURE JUSTICE

For Alice Parkinson

Editor, "The Maoriland Worker,"—I am sure most of your readers will be of one opinion regarding the terrible sentence imposed on the unfortunate girl Alice May Parkinson, and I am glad to see an agitation has already been started for her early release. Such an agitation, however, cannot be conducted without funds, and I am sure there are many of your readers who would be glad to subscribe to such a fund if given an opportunity. I therefore trust you will see your way to open a fund for the above purpose, to which I herewith subscribe five shillings.—Yours, etc.,

C.E.R.

"The Worker" has much pleasure in acceding to C.E.R.'s request, and we shall be glad to receive and acknowledge subscriptions for the "Alice Parkinson Release Fund."

ALICE PARKINSON RELEASE FUND.

	£	s.	d.
C.E.R.	0	5	0

on a table so that the photo almost suggests she is standing in the dock, but her clothes are not those she wore for her trial; it is more likely that the photo came from earlier and happier times in her life. The *Maoriland Worker* acknowledged that the block for the photo had been 'kindly lent' by NZ *Truth*; the two weekly newspapers almost certainly collaborated to some extent on the Alice Parkinson campaign.

Already, fund-raising for Alice had begun. In a letter to the *Maoriland Worker*, CER[8] suggested that many readers would be glad to contribute money to a fund for Alice and asked that the newspaper set up such a fund. CER subscribed five shillings. The *Maoriland Worker* was happy to oblige and announced that it would receive and acknowledge subscriptions for the Alice Parkinson Release Fund. CER's five shillings was the first donation.[9] A collection gathered as people filed out of the big Picture Palace meeting netted £3/17/2.

The campaign was on its way. More and more women were

joining in the protests for Alice. Her case, involving as it did socially taboo elements of female sexual licence, as well as murder and betrayal, had engrossed members of the public and especially women, who had packed the Napier courthouse to follow her trial and appeal. Now, sustained publicity throughout June and July in *Truth* and the *Maoriland Worker* was stirring many women's groups into action. It was likely that many of these women saw some of their own unacknowledged concerns around pregnancy and marriage, some of their own fears and frustrations in Alice's story. Women from all over New Zealand were writing to these papers to offer what help they could.

Sarah A Bradley wrote from St Albans in Christchurch 'If you send me a form, I will do all I can to help you, I have already 9s. 6d. in hand with a promise of more …' As the war was on everyone's minds, Mrs Bradley continues: '… In today's *Times* we see a V.C. has been presented to a soldier for killing seven of his fellow beings, and this poor creature gets jail for life for killing one being who had driven her no doubt to desperation …'[10]

'Mother of a large family', who no doubt had problems of her own, wrote in from Wellington:

> … When Powelka[11] was sentenced to 20 years, all N.Z. cried aloud, and they made a great cry of it; but he was a man. Now, sir, the day may come when the doors of the iron gates swing open and this girl may realise there are true Christian friends still alive in this beautiful land of ours.[12]

Women's groups as well as individual women were supporting the movement. The Women's Section of the Social Democratic Party took the lead by sending a circular to women's organisations in Wellington and invited their representatives to a meeting. This gathering was well attended and participants were enthusiastic for the cause.[13] Jane Donaldson, secretary of the Release Alice Parkinson campaign, gave a strong speech. As Harry Holland did at the People's Picture Palace, she used the protest to focus interest on some of the wider concerns for women. She hoped the day would come when there would be women on all juries

A WOMAN WRONGED

Being by way of comment on the harsh sentence imposed on Alice Parkinson, the young woman sentenced to imprisonment for the term of her natural life for shooting her false lover.

Scorned by the man whose babe I bore,
Who left me outcast, neither maid nor wife;
On whom I'd blindly spent my scanty store,
Fondly believing I should share his life;
Desperate, distraught, half mad with grief and shame,
I shot that man—was I to blame?

Blinded by love, I suffered each rebuff,
Foolishly thinking love would grow again;
By kith and kin abhorred, my path was rough,
But little cared I, buoyed by love's fierce flame.
When disillusion came—a dark day dawned,
Hell has no fury like a woman scorned.

And then that man-made law which men call just,
That law unsentimental, uninspired,
Opened its pond'rous tomes all thick with dust,
And on me wreaked the vengeance it desired.
In gaol I have to languish all my life.
Oh, pity me!—a mother but no wife.

Picture and poem anonymously sent to *Truth*.
The text is reproduced in the appendix on page 102.

where women were being tried, and women on all public bodies, including parliament. Jane Donaldson also contrasted the lenient sentences given to men for gross offences against little children with the sentence imposed on Alice. More women spoke briefly to the meeting and all were in favour of the cause. It was hoped that women in other centres would take the matter up and hold similar gatherings. The assembled women agreed formally to hold a large public meeting of protest at an early date. The women were so confident of the rightness of their cause that they agreed to ask the mayor of Wellington, John Pearce Luke, for the free use of the Town Hall for the occasion. He turned them down.

Not everyone at this time was wholeheartedly in favour of Alice's release from gaol. 'M.G.' no doubt spoke for a large section of the public when he or she reminded readers of Wellington's *Evening Post* that: '... we must remember that the murdered boy West is 6ft under the ground. And there is no release for him', and:

> I see no reason why Alice Parkinson could not have made a fresh start after her confinement was well over, as so many others have had to do, especially as her child was dead. Any love she may have had for West was also dead. Having discovered that he was 'a rotten cur' (her own words) why should she insist on becoming his wife? ...[14]

But the mood of the country was generally for Alice, rather than against her, and the agitation to reduce her sentence or to free her altogether was spreading. In a letter to the Women's Christian Temperance journal, *The White Ribbon*, Emily Gibson, Honourable Secretary of the Auckland Women's Political League, called on the members of the Temperance Union to support Alice, and they did this in increasing numbers. Emily Gibson even drew on Portia from Shakespeare's *Merchant of Venice* to support her cause:

> Though justice be thy plea, consider this,
> That in the course of justice none of us
> Should see salvation.[15]

Since its founding in New Zealand the Women's Christian Temperance Union had concerned itself not only with crusades against liquor but also with issues of law, human rights and prison reform. It had become a force to be reckoned with. Branches as far apart as Mataura, Ngaere and Pahiatua and many others petitioned the government to have Alice freed from gaol. This support from the WCTU provided the campaign with respectability and clout.

Most of the energies of the Release Alice Parkinson Committee were going into planning the big Town Hall protest meeting advertised for the evening of Thursday 16 September 1915. Barney Dolan, Alice's lawyer, had willingly agreed to speak to the meeting, and Harry Holland, Jane Donaldson and others would also address the crowd. A Watersiders' Band would play selections of music from 7pm when the doors first opened, until 8pm when the meeting was to begin. There would be a collection at the door.

As chance would have it, the Thursday night of the meeting was one of the stormiest and roughest in Wellington's history. The rain poured down and the wind shrieked and howled around the building, making it hard for the audience to hear. It was difficult to estimate just how many people turned up for the meeting. On the next day the *Maoriland Worker* estimated between eight hundred and a thousand 'at least', but the *Evening Post*, never an enthusiastic supporter of Alice, estimated the number at three to four hundred. The true number of attendees on such a miserable night was probably somewhere in between.

Barney Dolan addressed the meeting for three quarters of an hour. Over the racket of the weather outside he reminded his listeners that in New Zealand there was no right, as there was in England, of appeal against a sentence and argued in favour of the establishment of a Court of Criminal Appeal in this country. He reminded his hearers that Alice was '… one of the best little girls in the Sunday School … ' and remembered to praise some of the many newspapers who were also supporting the campaign. *Truth*, the *New Zealand Times*, the *Maoriland Worker*, the *Wairarapa*

Harry Holland, 1922.
1/1-018348-F. Alexander Turnbull Library

Age, the *Auckland Star*, the *Christchurch Star* and several West Coast papers were all helping to keep Alice's name in the public eye. The meeting ended with a resolution protesting at the severity of Alice's sentence and calling on the Minister of Justice to take steps to shorten her time in gaol and thus gave effect to the strong recommendation of her jury. Unsurprisingly, it was carried unanimously.[16] By now more than sixty thousand people had signed the big petition. Considering the small size of the New Zealand population at that time it was a remarkable number. Indeed it would have been hard to avoid being badgered to sign the petition while out on the streets in Wellington at that point; and this gives a sense of the determination of Alice's campaigners.

Support was flowing in from men as well as women. Petition forms arrived signed by 'one hundred and seventy-five men from one of New Zealand's warships', with a note that this represented ninety percent of the ship's company.[17] In a letter to *Truth* entitled 'A Soldier's Tribute', a 'Liverpool's Own' soldier encamped at the Showgrounds in Palmerston North wrote that there was not a man in the camp who would not willingly sign the petition and 'take Miss Alice Parkinson as a "Mascot" for we reckon she is a heroine'.[18] Even Grey Lynn's Carpenters and Joiners' Union — in an industry not readily given to political activism — signed up for the cause.

Articles about Alice and her plight in *Truth* and the *Maoriland Worker* touched the hearts of New Zealanders. In July 1915 a man from Wanganui (*Truth* protected his identity) wrote: 'I personally know this young lady and may say that at any time hereafter, I would only be too pleased to make her my own wife.'[19] Some individuals sent her fruit and sweets but it was doubtful if she was ever permitted to receive any of these.

Requests for printed petition forms were still pouring into *Truth*'s Wellington, Christchurch and Auckland offices, but by September *Truth* was calling for the sheaves of signed forms to be returned by no later than the 20th so that they could be presented to His Excellency the Governor in Council by Barney Dolan in early October, as arranged. On 7 October a petition with the same wording as the first was also presented to the Speaker and the House of Representatives. All those who had worked so hard for the Release Alice Parkinson campaign were now riding high, and Jane Donaldson wrote to *Truth* to thank them for all their efforts on Alice's behalf.[20] Surely now a reduction in her sentence, or even her freedom from gaol, was only a matter of time. But nothing was ever that easy.

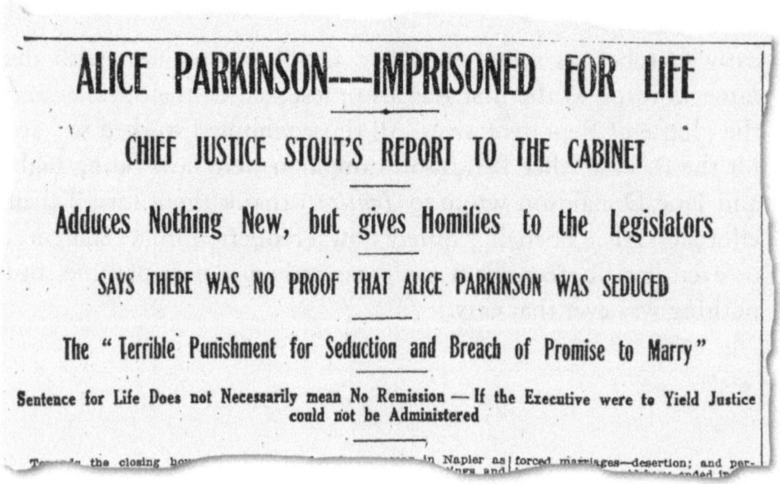

ALICE PARKINSON---IMPRISONED FOR LIFE

CHIEF JUSTICE STOUT'S REPORT TO THE CABINET

Adduces Nothing New, but gives Homilies to the Legislators

SAYS THERE WAS NO PROOF THAT ALICE PARKINSON WAS SEDUCED

The "Terrible Punishment for Seduction and Breach of Promise to Marry"

Sentence for Life Does not Necessarily mean No Remission — If the Executive were to Yield Justice could not be Administered

NZ Truth[1]

EIGHT

Despair

The campaigners for Alice had reckoned without Chief Justice Sir Robert Stout.

In response to the general agitation for Alice's release, Stout had been asked to furnish a long and thorough report on her case. He completed it on 22 September 1915 and it was delivered to the Department of Justice and placed before parliament.

Stout was a well-known eugenist thinker and a member of the small but far-reaching Eugenics Education Society founded in New Zealand five years earlier in 1910. He believed, as did many other prominent eugenists of the period both in Europe and New Zealand, that society was threatened from the outside by non-white races and from the inside by 'the unfit', the drunkard, the criminal and the mentally ill.[2] Several prison administrators of the time were also eugenists. Stout believed in the existence of a criminal class and the

Sir Robert Stout

inheritance of criminal instincts.[3] '... There was a criminal class which was just as distinct among humanity as a bulldog is amongst dogs ... '[4] Alice's father was a reformed drunkard, and examples of her language read to the court were vulgar and 'unwomanly': '... It will pay you better to shut your mouth, you old cow ...' or '... You rotten cur ...' It was apparent in Stout's report that he saw Alice, despite her respectable churchgoing family and her good work history, as a menace to society and a member of one of the criminal classes who should be locked away for society's good and her own reform.

Stout's *Report of the Chief Justice* was in tiny print and made hard reading.[5] His first paragraph said that he could not, in passing sentence, accept the recommendation of Alice's jury because:

1. The killing was deliberate, having been previously threatened and planned.
2. There was in fact no provocation.
3. If the jury had acted according to the strict law and the evidence, they ought to have found Alice guilty of murder.

Stout's report was blunt. He pointed out that Alice had 'kept up an illicit connection with the deceased for about two years' and he considered she '... must have kept bad company in Napier, for the words she uses in her letters show acquaintance with slang and the seamy side of our social life ...' He summed up:

> ... To allow a person, male or female, who thinks he or she has been wronged to inflict punishment without trial, by private assassination, would be such a violation of law and order that no civilised community could submit to it. It is far worse than lynch law ...

and '... Wherever private assassination is allowed in a community without punishment civilisation vanishes and moral degeneration sets in ...' It was clear there would be no mercy for Alice from Stout's quarter. In his opinion she did not deserve it.

Looking at it now, Chief Justice Stout's trenchant account of Alice's character and the magnitude of her offence must have influenced the Committee appointed to re-examine her case. What else did they have to go on? In the end, in the matter of Report Number 220 — Petition of CLARA E. RAE and others of Wellington, praying for clemency and for a reduction of the sentence passed on one Alice May Parkinson the members of the Parliamentary Petitions Committee M to Z had no recommendation to make and merely asked that the report by the Chief Justice be attached to their own report and that the whole thing be printed.[6] This was a vast disappointment for all those individuals who had worked so hard to release Alice Parkinson, and for a while the campaign lost momentum.

It was not clear how much Alice herself knew about all this controversy. Since her arrest and trial she had constantly been featured in newspapers, been discussed in countless kitchens and on street corners and been talked about in parliament. Nevertheless, shut away in Addington, with few visitors and a letter from her family only once a month, she might have known very little. And the New Zealand public who felt they knew everything about her, in reality did not know much. Her whereabouts were seldom mentioned in the papers. At least one letter writer to a Wellington paper firmly believed that Alice was being held in Wellington Gaol and went on in print to imagine her daily life as a convict 'buried away' behind those forbidding doors.[7]

Meanwhile, away in Addington Reformatory, Alice was struggling to settle in. The reports on her in the prison files are scanty, but those that do exist show that she had a quick temper, and she could draw on a rich supply of abusive or threatening language if she came into any sort of conflict with other inmates. It was her way of getting by. There was also an 'episode' with knives first hinted at but then denied at one of the Wellington women's protest meetings.[8] She was occasionally isolated from other prisoners and sent to work in the prison gardens.

Alice had other deeper problems in these early days at Addington: she was suffering from excruciating headaches. From the time of Bert's ultimate rejection she had always planned not just to kill him but to kill herself as well. In her unhappy state she could see no other solution to her problems and distress. But although Bert was mortally wounded by the bullets she fired into his body, the one she fired point-blank into her own temple did not kill her, and so she had to live on to take the consequences for her actions. It was a cruel irony. In all the reports of her behaviour at her trial and sentencing she seems to be 'glazed' or 'dazed' and not taking much in. It was likely that the bullet, lodged deep in her brain, had contributed to this confusion and was still causing her migraines several months later.

Time was passing. Through 1916 and 1917 the Release Alice Parkinson Committee members were still meeting, though not as often as before, and they were still trying to keep Alice's name before the public. If she was aware of it at all, this must have been heartening for her. But the ever present war news, the grief over casualties and deaths and the need to maintain public cheerfulness and high morale in the midst of so much misery meant that those who supported her previously had less time and energy to do so now. Both Alice and the campaign were at a low ebb.

Despite this, *Truth* made sure that its readers did not forget her. Its Christchurch reporters now and then made enquiries 'to the

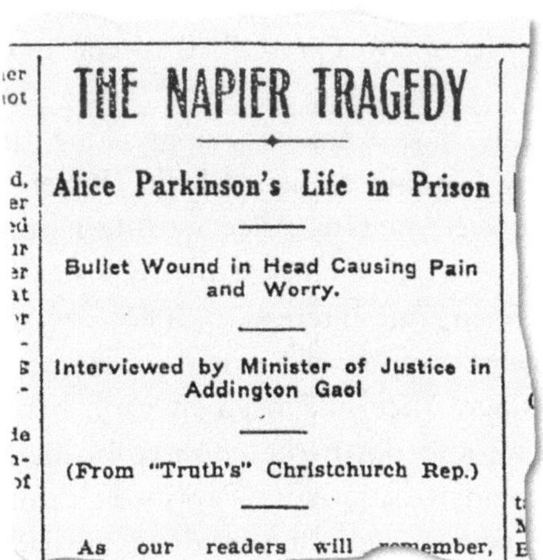

THE NAPIER TRAGEDY

Alice Parkinson's Life in Prison

Bullet Wound in Head Causing Pain and Worry.

Interviewed by Minister of Justice in Addington Gaol

(From "Truth's" Christchurch Rep.)

As our readers will remember,

proper quarters', almost certainly the matron of the Reformatory, Mrs McBryde. *Truth* was told that Alice's conduct was very good. She was 'one of the most exemplary of prisoners, not only causing her gaolers no worry, but being of very material assistance to them in many ways.' However, of late 'it has been noticed that she has been growing more and more moody and apparently preoccupied, and that her general health was becoming affected.' The prison spokesperson told *Truth* that lately Alice had been very reserved and uncomplaining: '... She appeared to have made up her mind to "see it through" and to give as little trouble as she could to those in authority around her.'[9]

Truth also told its readers of Alice's painful headaches and said they were getting worse.[10]

With her long sentence and so much interest in her from members of the public, Alice was always going to be something of a special prisoner. Thus, in June 1917 when Josiah Hanan, the Minister of Justice, and Charles Matthews, Chief Inspector of Prisons, made an official visit to Addington her case was put before them. Hanan then had a special interview with Alice herself. He later requested that her head be x-rayed and that the prison medical officer do all he could to find out the seat of the trouble and remove the cause. Sadly the bullet was found to be in the ossian centre of Alice's brain and too far in for the surgeons of the day to remove. She was prescribed spectacles to help with the headaches.[11]

In prison the days were wearyingly long. In August 1918 Salvation Army Captain Emily Isabelle (Belle) Parkinson, who had been permitted to visit Alice in Addington, wrote to the authorities, 'I see a great change in my sister. She is growing hopeless and losing all interest in life.'[12] Members of Alice's family had always supported her and would continue to do so. In the years since Alice had been in gaol, her father, George, had travelled up and down the country in his Salvation Army uniform to attend Release Alice Parkinson campaign meetings, and Isabella Parkinson's love for her daughter had never wavered.

Blanche Baughan.
Clifford Photo, an23185494,
National Library of Australia.

When George Parkinson died in 1919, Alice was devastated. She was not permitted to travel to Hawke's Bay to visit her dying father or to attend his funeral.

However, as time passed at Addington Reformatory, there were fewer reports of Alice flying into a temper over trifles as she did at first. Her cell was scrupulously tidy. She was more settled and worked hard. Perhaps by now some of the trauma over the death of Bert West and her lost child was fading. Perhaps now she was showing more signs of the cheerful and trusted friend she once was, the helpful domestic servant described by her past employers in court and vouched for by them in letters to *Truth* and to the prison authorities.[13] And she was not without friends in prison. From around 1917 or 1918 onwards Alice was regularly being visited by a woman who already featured in New Zealand literary history and who would go on to be a significant prison reformer in this country.[14] Born in Surrey, England, in 1870, Blanche Edith Baughan graduated from Royal Holloway College London with a first-class honours degree in Classics. She first arrived in New Zealand in 1900 and by the time she came into contact with Alice she was already a skilled writer who had published at least one collection of poetry. She wrote poetry and short 'sketches' in down-to-earth everyday language about ordinary unpretentious people. In an era when poems especially were often written in elevated or 'poetic' language, this was a welcome change, and she was recognised for it. She also wrote a number of widely published travel guides both to well-known travel destinations and to some of the more remote regions of New Zealand. She was a mountaineer and tramper. At the time she first met Alice she was a living in a cottage at the top of Clifton Spur in Sumner, near Christchurch.

Blanche was a woman of principle and determination. She would have first came into contact with prison authorities around 1917 when she used her home to shelter a couple of young women absconders.[15] The authorities were less than pleased, but Blanche was not deterred. She believed that prison officers should be more than just gaolers, that the prison system should encourage the self-respect of prisoners, who should be reformed rather than merely punished for their crimes. Blanche began to visit Alice regularly and became an official visitor to the institution, so was visiting other long-stay inmates there as well. It was likely she saw in Alice something of the younger woman's inner despair, and also realised that Alice still had the chance of being rehabilitated into a blameless life if only she could be set free. In some of Blanche Baughan's carefully worded letters to the Prisons Board regarding Alice, we have a chance to get closer to Alice herself — to see how she really appeared to someone who was visiting her frequently. '... Morally, I am quite certain that she is doing her best. As I read her nature, it is that of a woman in whom the affections are deep and strong, and in whom the outraging of these has worked havoc ...' and also, '... But I do know that she makes continual efforts to conquer the temper that helped to cause the crime, that she responds to every effort one makes towards understanding her, and that she is extremely susceptible to kindness ... '[16] give an indication of a woman who was at least trying to put the past behind her and get by.

Blanche Baughan would continue to support Alice, as did her Napier lawyer. Barney Dolan was still convinced that she had a rough deal and had never given up on her. In a 1903 Australian case strikingly similar to Alice's, Ethel Herringe had shot the father of her illegitimate child in a hotel room in Cowra, New South Wales, but had been sentenced to only two and a half years in gaol and had been released even before this after pressure from the Australian public.[17] But as 1918 turned to 1919 and then to 1920 it seemed that no matter who lined up in her corner to support her release, the New Zealand Justice Department and prison authorities would never let Alice go, and that in her case a life sentence really did mean life.

NINE

The free air of God's Own Country

In 1919 the protests over Alice Parkinson's case intensified once more. The war was finished, the battered soldiers had come home to their farms and families, and the brutal influenza epidemic that followed the war had finally run its course. There was more time again to work for causes such as Alice's. While the men had been away fighting overseas, women had worked hard to keep farms and households running. They had a renewed confidence in their own abilities to get things fixed.

The members of the Wellington Labour Women's Release Alice Parkinson Campaign Committee were still meeting, and in April 1919 they formed a deputation to the Minister of Justice, Thomas Wilford, urging him to release Alice Parkinson from 'durance vile'. Jane Donaldson was the first speaker. She had fought determinedly for Alice, and she did not give up lightly. She explained to Wilford that the deputation had come to see if a move could be made in the direction of granting a pardon for Alice, who had now served nearly four years in prison. She and the other women in the deputation ran through the particulars of Alice's case with Wilford and suggested that as part of the general national rejoicing at the end of the war, Alice should be permitted to '... once more walk out of prison a free woman to enjoy the free air of God's Own Country.'[1] A further speaker told

Thomas Mason Wilford, 1928.
1/1-018737-F Alexander Turnbull Library.

Wilford that her son had worked with Bert West in the railway workshops in Napier and that on the night Alice had arranged to meet West 'at the Manse with the special licence, [for the marriage] West went to the workshops and laughingly told his workmates where she was waiting and said she would have to wait a long time for him.'[2] Bert West is a rather shadowy figure in all the records of Alice's story, so it is good to catch a glimpse of him here, although nearly five years after the event this was a second-hand account.

Wilford listened to the deputation but told them again that offenders must pay the penalty for their disobedience. He said that he deplored the fact that there was no Court of Appeal in New Zealand. If there had been one, Alice could have had her sentence reviewed by a bench of judges and not just by Stout alone. Wilford was soon bringing in a bill to parliament to enable convicted persons to have the right to have their cases reheard by a Court of Appeal. He hoped it would be passed soon. This was just a crumb of comfort. The deputation to the Minister of Justice had a good hearing, but went home empty-handed.

In the years thus far, much of the pressure to have Alice released from gaol had come from the Wellington region. Now the women of Auckland began to put real energy into the campaign. By the beginning of 1920 there were so many efforts to have Alice Parkinson freed that it is hard to keep track of all of them. It had become clear that Alice's supporters were not going to go away; in fact support for her cause was still growing. The Auckland Women's International and Political League was a group of Labour women who were concerned with women's issues and with national and international issues of equality and justice.[3] At their meeting on 10 February 1920 they passed a resolution that the government release Alice Parkinson and also that a regulation be made that '... in common with other public servants all judges, including the Chief Justice, be superannuated upon reaching a certain age, the age to be fixed by Parliament at its next session.'[4] This was a dig at Sir Robert Stout, who was 71 years old when he

Arthur William de Brito Savile Foljambe, 2nd Earl of Liverpool. First Governor-General of New Zealand (1917-1920).
G15166-1/1 Alexander Turnbull Library

sentenced Alice. He had by now reached the age of 76 and was still in office.

In May 1920 another huge petition circulated throughout the Dominion. The organisers collected over a hundred thousand signatures and presented these to Lord Liverpool, the Governor-General, along with a request that he pass the petition on to the Prince of Wales who was visiting New Zealand. It was felt that where nothing else had worked, a royal pardon from the prince might open the doors of Alice's gaol and set her free. But Alice remained in Addington.

The release committee was undeterred. On 16 June 1920 *Truth* reported that the Alice Parkinson case had again been considered by the government. By now it had received 'numerous' petitions and resolutions concerning Alice and the harshness of her sentence. *Truth* wrote that today the Cabinet had decided on legislation that would allow Alice's case and others like it to be considered by the Prisons Board. This board would have the power to recommend to the Governor-General the release on probation of Alice Parkinson.

The members of the Release Alice Parkinson Committee now scented victory. Together with the Auckland Women's International and Political League and other supporters, they went on to organise what was described as a 'monster' meeting on 27 June at the Globe Theatre in Auckland. A lyric string band would be there to entertain those who attended. There were a thousand people at this meeting. At its close the Auckland citizens voted to call on the government to pass the Prisons Board and probation legislation at present under consideration by the House. In addition, the meeting urged the government to pass a Criminal Appeal Bill giving prisoners such as Alice a chance to appeal in cases where a judge overrode a jury's strong recommendation to mercy.[5] Release Alice Parkinson campaigners sent this resolution to the Minister of Justice and to every Member of Parliament.[6]

They kept the pressure on. On 6 September 1920 the secretary Edward Stevenson, a builder from Mount Albert Road, was writing to the Controller General of Prisons: 'Scarcely a day passes that I have not got one or more enquiries about Alice Parkinson ... would you kindly let me know if your prison Reform Bill has finally passed. I would be pleased to be able to tell them if the Prisons Board now have the power to review her case.'

This perseverance was paying off. Three days later Ernest Lee, who had taken over as Minister of Justice in April that year, replied to Stevenson that the Crimes Amendment Bill had now passed the legislature. It could have been an occasion for rejoicing, but for the fact that Alice was still not free. Nevertheless, hopes were high for her speedy release from gaol, and Stevenson wrote to the board to assure them that: 'should this unfortunate woman be given another chance in life nothing would be done to make a heroine of her.'[7]

Even the staff at Addington Reformatory now supported Alice's release. In her gaoler's report Matron McBryde wrote:

> I may without hesitation say that I do not expect this woman to again break the law sufficiently to bring herself within its reach. During the past five and a half years her experiences of physical and mental suffering have not been lost as lessons of self-control.[8]

and Acting Superintendent Ellen Hunt commented: 'She is a good clean worker, and does what she can to help and is never idle.'[9]

Alice Parkinson's case duly came before the Prisons Board, and in February 1921 they met to consider the matter. Unfortunately, the case was declined. The Board considered itself not warranted in recommending her release on account of her crime and of her conduct in gaol. It was likely they did not want to be seen to give in too easily. Alice had committed a shocking crime and there were still members of the community who felt she must suffer and be fully punished for it. But the members of the Prisons Board did leave the door open, if just a small amount. In a report on the case Charles Matthews, the Controller General of Prisons, commented that if Alice's conduct improved '... the Board would be enabled to recommend probation, but that such a recommendation would entirely depend on her conduct and on her proved control of herself and her actions.'[10]

The uncertainty over her case must have been frustrating for Alice, though. Early in January 1921 she had a small run-in with one of the prison officers but had been merely admonished and discharged. Matron McBryde reported that 'This woman must be losing heart some what. She is a good general or cook' and added 'I do not think she will again transgress the law.'[11] From the outside it seemed like a stalemate, but in reality efforts were now going on within the justice system itself to have Alice freed. Blanche Baughan, from Sumner, Mrs F O Smith from Richmond, and Mrs A Millar from Lyttelton, were trusted official visitors to Addington and all three visited inmates regularly, especially those women serving longer sentences. In July 1921 Charles Matthews asked the three women to report to the Prisons Board on Alice's present condition, her likelihood of re-offending and her possible future behaviour. The women were asked to comment jointly on whether they thought Alice should be released on probation, and their reasons for this opinion. In the end, the women sent three separate reports. Blanche Baughan in particular wrote a compassionate letter to the Prisons Board. She had constantly supported Alice, and had been in touch with Barney Dolan and with Alice's mother, Isabella, in Tikokino:

> … To her widowed mother she is devoted, and the mother is devoted to her. A letter addressed to myself by the latter says, 'I would be only too pleased to have her home with me. She would be a great help in helping to look after myself and housework. … I hope … all her brothers and sisters with myself will be able to welcome her to her home again … She would be a blessing to me … '[12]

In her report Blanche Baughan considered that further punishment would only be detrimental for Alice's state of mind and 'moral progress', whereas a normal domestic and home life would give her the very best outcome possible. Blanche Baughan's opinion to the Prisons Board spoke strongly for Alice's release, and it is probable that the other two reports were in similar vein for Constable Hugh Snow, from the Waipawa Police in Hawke's Bay, was asked to check in Tikokino on whether Alice had a suitable home to be released into.

Constable Snow sent back a glowing report on Alice's family. He wrote that Isabella Parkinson was a 'respectable hard-working industrious woman, highly respected in this district.' There were also 'several sons working in the district all of which were hard-working industrious young men.'[13] Slowly, the ground was being prepared for Alice's release. On 21 July she herself wrote a rare letter to Barney Dolan and thanked him for remembering her. She was still suffering from severe headaches and would for the rest of her life, but her room was most comfortable, she told Dolan, and it was owing to this she had been able to keep up. She went on to say 'I am allowed visitors and have formed many kind friendships here. I have deeply regretted my many mistakes ... ' In a telling paragraph Alice also adds:

> ... The one thing that has caused me bitter sorrow is the cruel letter I wrote to Mrs West and I know I made her very unhappy. I have worried many times and feel the great wrong I did her. When I think of my life and the sadness I have brought into it, I can hardly bear it at times ... [14]

On 23 July Barney Dolan also wrote to the Prisons Board requesting the release of Alice Parkinson on probation. For the past six years Alice's life had been ship-wrecked. Now, it seemed, she might get a chance to start again. Comments about her at this time indicated that she was putting up a 'brave fight' and that she was learning lessons of self-control in a very hard school.

Page six of the *Evening Post* of 27 August 1921 had the modest headline:

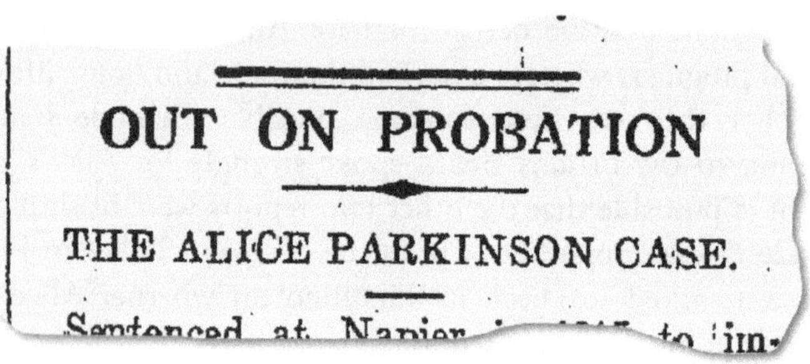

OUT ON PROBATION

THE ALICE PARKINSON CASE.

Sentenced at Napier

The *Post* told its readers that the Prisons Board had met and recommended Alice Parkinson be released on probationary conditions and that this had been approved by the Governor-General. *Truth*, as one of the papers that never stopped fighting for Alice, was far more self-congratulatory.

Truth had a right to be pleased with all the effort its editor, Robert Hogg, and other journalists put into the campaign. Social historian Redmer Yska writes 'the publicity ensured talk of the Parkinson case reached from North Cape to Bluff. It was an

FREE AT LAST

ALICE PARKINSON RELEASED

Another Triumph For "Truth"

PEOPLE'S PAPER DELUGED WITH CONGRATULATIONS

example of *Truth*'s growing power to transform a regional story into a national phenomenon. Importantly, it put Truth on the map as a populist paper on the side of the "plugs" or workers.'[15]

The long *Truth* article covered yet again Alice's trial and sentence, Dolan's appeal, Wilford's bill, the mass meetings, the huge petitions and the efforts from women's organisations throughout New Zealand to have Alice set free. From early on the morning of Saturday 27 August, congratulations to Alice Parkinson and *Truth* were beginning to pour into the *Truth* office. The paper proudly saw it as a triumph for *itself*, as well as for mercy and justice. The newspaper article also urged its readers to remember all of the other 'earnest workers for this cause … All did their "bit" and now that Alice Parkinson was once more a free woman they, like *Truth* must have felt that their efforts had been amply rewarded.'[16]

Away from all of the fanfare, Alice Parkinson passed quietly through Wellington. She was on her way back to the sanctuary of her mother's home in Tikokino, and would stay out of the eye of the public for the rest of her life.

Part Two

ALICE PARKINSON
WITH HARD LABOUR
The Case of Alice Parkinson
A new play by Carol Markwell
Directed by Phillip Mann and Jo Kahl
Stage 2, 17–20 November
Book at Suter Gallery
Supported by the Nelson Provincial Arts Council
& the Arts Council of New Zealand Toi Aotearoa

TEN

Finding Alice

Stories work in curious ways. Alice Parkinson's story has become part of New Zealand history and folklore. Things cluster to it. It is a strand in the much larger story that we tell ourselves, a pattern of threads and colours that we are constantly making, unpicking and then remaking. Here is my part in it.

For two or three years in the early 1990s I spent a lot of time thinking about and searching for Alice Parkinson. I was (and still am) interested in local stories and in writing plays that bring the people in these old stories alive once more — to put them into the light and celebrate them so that they are not just figures in some forgotten history book but are real and believable human beings. Individuals of flesh and blood who are passionate and sad and excited and greedy and forgetful, just as we all are.

The year before, in 1991, I had finished a Nelson community play and had seen the wholehearted response from local audiences when one of 'their' stories was being performed.[1] So I was keen to write another community play. I was looking for a play that would involve a large cast of women as well as men — one that would show how ordinary New Zealand people (and especially women) can combine and work together willingly for a common cause.

I was at a summertime party in Nelson when a friend asked what the topic of my next play was going to be. I said, rather unhelpfully, that I didn't know. He said 'Have you thought of Alice Parkinson?' and that started me on a long quest which has continued to this day. I had no idea who Alice was, but decided to look for whatever I could find of this young woman and of her story.

At first there was very little. I found a few lines written about her here and there, then a longer piece in an illustrated New Zealand history book.[2] Not much to go on, at that point, but Alice, and her drastic way of solving her problems, shone out from the pages. She was a gift to any playwright, but also an enigma. Who was she — a villain, a stroppy heroine or simply a struggling survivor? And where did she come from? Did she ever marry? What happened to her after gaol? I was intrigued by Alice and her story and determined to find out, but it was never going to be easy. At this stage I had only an old Mac Plus computer with a dot matrix printer and no access to the internet. If I wanted to learn any more of Alice, I would have to go to the National Library in Wellington.

I made a short trip across Cook Strait and on a rainy morning put my coat and bag in a locker and climbed hopefully up the stairs of the big building to look at the collection of old newspapers held there on microfilm. Reel by reel I searched the inky pages of the labour weekly, the *Maoriland Worker*. Eventually, after a few false starts, I found what I was looking for. Wednesday by Wednesday from early 1915 onwards there were bold black headlines about Alice. There in front of me were the meetings, petitions, appeals for funds, deputations to government. I copied as much detail as I could and took smudgy photocopies of the eye-wateringly tiny print wherever possible. Somehow, reading these papers of the day made Alice more real. This was history, but now it was close to me — just a hair's breadth away.

That trip was the first of many. I came to enjoy working in the busy National Library with its helpful librarians, its hushed voices, the scratch of pencils (never pens) on paper and the cheerful basement café where I sometimes took a break from work. I searched other newspapers too. Slowly, gradually, I was piecing together what Alice had done and what had happened to her as a result. Especially in the local papers, there were detailed accounts of her killing of Bert West and of her trial and appeal in Napier. Some of the papers had printed Alice's abusive and tormented letters to Bert and his mother in full. Her increasing despair after her baby died was becoming more and more apparent. It was almost too much information. But for the next few weeks, whenever I could, I searched in the library, looking for whatever might help me understand what had propelled Alice into taking the desperate steps she did. I still had no real idea of where she had come from — she seemed to exist only in the pages of the newspapers and in an isolated bubble of time. Perhaps she had some living descendants I could talk to who might link her to the present day? I set out to look for any who were out there.

1993 was Women's Suffrage Year in New Zealand. Because so many different women's groups had worked together to try to free Alice from gaol I applied to the Women's Suffrage Celebrations committee and they made a small grant to enable me to do further research. This meant I could afford to take my car on the ferry from Picton to Wellington and then go on to Alice's birthplace in Hawke's Bay.

With high hopes my artist friend Janice Gill and I duly set off. We went first to what was becoming familiar territory to me, the National Library. Over the previous weeks I had searched many records and papers to see if I could find if Alice had ever married. Now with Janice's help I had another try. I had earlier found George Parkinson's 1919 obituary with all of her brothers and sisters mentioned by name, but Alice was still recorded as 'Miss'. Now, together, we located Isabella Parkinson's obituary of 1928. It too had all the surviving siblings' names printed, and this time the sisters' names were given in full. One by one we ticked off Alice's sisters' names and paired them with their married surnames: Clara, Evelyn, Ruby, Ruth, Emily. There was just one name that did not match up. It was 'Mrs O'Loughlin'. She must have married and become an O'Loughlin! Janice and I were elated. We had found Alice! To celebrate this discovery we bought cheese and biscuits and a bottle of wine. But we still had a long way to go.

We drove through the winding Manawatu Gorge and on through the Takapau Plains. We were heading for Tikokino, the

The Parkinsons' house in Tikokino.

central Hawke's Bay village of Alice's childhood. Perhaps there was a surviving family member who would remember Alice's story. The Parkinson house was still there — a tiny abode for a family of so many, but with a certain olde-worlde charm. The cottage had a peaked roof in the traditional way and a rambling garden. A small verandah ran along the front. On the road outside Janice pulled out her sketch book and began to sketch the carved wooden verandah posts. I started to walk through the gate. An elderly woman with long white hair came out to see us.[3] I told her who we were and asked if we could speak with her for a while. She was very definite in her reply.

'No,' she said. She would not talk to us. There was nothing she wished to say about Alice Parkinson.

It was disappointing, but we must accept that this was a sensitive subject and that she had every right not to talk about it. No one else we found had any knowledge of Alice, so we drove on to look at the graves in the cemetery just out of the township. Perhaps the dead sleeping there would yield up local stories far more eloquently than the living had so far. Suddenly the car gave a tremendously loud bang and slewed to the side. I pulled over and stopped. The rear tyre was flat and had a bar of shiny metal sticking out of it, possibly lost from some kind of machinery. 'Tikokino's revenge', we joked as we eventually drove on to Napier. In Art Deco Napier we looked at the Masonic Hotel, where Alice first worked as a pantrymaid, and walked along Nelson Crescent where she shot Bert West. Although post-earthquake Napier was much changed from Alice's day, somehow the past seemed very close when we looked at the places where she lived and worked. I had already established that Joy Axford, the curator of archives from the Hawke's Bay Museum, who grew up in Tikokino, had never heard of Alice Parkinson. Perhaps there was still a conspiracy of silence around her. Janice sketched some of the Art Deco buildings in the central city.[4] It was time to go home. We packed up and headed for Nelson.

Back home, I gathered my thoughts about Alice. I had a play to write and time was passing, but I still could not start on it. There were so many things about her story I wanted to look into more deeply. More and more I could see that what happened to Alice in 1914 and beyond was part of a much bigger New Zealand-wide story. It was a story of money and blood and family, and of how men treated women and women regarded men at this time. It was a tale of 'bad' women and 'good' women and I wondered whether these stereotypes still mattered to us. Alice's story concerned one individual, but it was also a far wider story of class and of gender, of tragedy and compassion. There was so much in it to explore that I hardly knew where to begin. In the end, I went back to Alice.

I still had so many questions about her. Alice was a loved member of her family, and her ex-employers testified that she was a liked and trusted hard-working hotel worker and domestic servant. What made her go off the rails after Bert refused to marry her? Why could she see no other alternative than to kill Bert and herself? And who was she? I found a number of Alice O'Loughlins in old electoral rolls; any one of them could now have been Alice. I made yet another trip from Nelson to Wellington.

This time I headed for the National Archives in Thorndon. This large building holds treasures such as the Treaty of Waitangi, and also early files and records from courts and other authorities from all around New Zealand. The records were safely stored away, so I needed to know what I was looking for before I could request to see it. However, the staff at Archives were friendly and helpful and after a few hiccoughs I was sitting with my pencil and paper in the big glass-walled reading room, searching through page after page of old Police and Justice Department files and ledgers. The room was quiet, with just the odd rustling of papers or readers getting up to carry records to and from their desks. Here again I had the sense that history was just under my fingertips. What came across most from these files was not how different from us the men and women of 'the past' were, but how alike. They complained, they got drunk, they were arrested and discharged, some prisoners trashed their cells, others ran away and were brought back reluctantly to gaol. Every one of the people who featured in these records was now long dead, as were the clerks and other officials who ruled the lines and entered their pen-and-ink comments into the big bound books. However, they still lived on, clamouring, disorderly, gossiping, righteous or sad, in the fading pages of those thousands of files and records.

It was so easy to get distracted here, in this room of busy silent readers, but I had a job to do. I was looking for Alice. What was it like for her in prison? How did she get on with the other prisoners? All the female inmates were there for longer than three months. At least now and then, they must have tested each other's nerves.

Eventually, I found Justice Department files dealing with Addington Reformatory. Matron Madeline McBryde featured in the records, and several visits of inspection of the prison by church groups and senior justice officials were noted and written up, as were various reports dealing with the causes of 'female crime'. This was all valuable background reading, but it still did not answer the central question I had around Alice. Why, why did she do it?

At last, after several visits to Archives I found something like the key to the riddle that was Alice. It was a typed report from Arthur Crosby, medical superintendent of Sunnyside Mental Hospital, dated 26 January 1921 and addressed to the Prisons Board.[5] Clearly the board was assessing Alice's suitability for release. Here, finally, is a compassionate report to the prison authorities which might do something to counter the damning report on Alice from Chief Justice Robert Stout, who had all along considered Alice was nothing more than a calculating and callous criminal.

Arthur Crosby's report considered Alice's mental state on the night of the tragedy, and first pointed out that she would have still been suffering from the loss of her child and her very recent confinement. He mentioned the effect Bert West's coolness and vacillating behaviour would have had on Alice and the fact that shortly before the killing she had been pushed to the ground by Bert's friend John Forde. This was familiar territory and had been covered at Alice's trial. However, Crosby went on to say 'In addition to this Parkinson's confinement was not a normal one. The presentation was a transverse one, requiring dismemberment of the child before delivery could be effected.'

I stared at this last sentence. What a brutal experience to undergo. Instead of the time and gentle nursing needed to recover from the bloody agony of her childbirth, Alice hurried to get herself discharged urgently from the nursing home because Bert had promised to marry her as soon as she did. The longed-for child was the link that would have kept Alice and Bert together. Now it was dead, and Bert did not want any more to do with her. It was not surprising that at this crucial time in her life Alice was angry and emotionally unstable. Crosby mentioned Alice's indignation at Bert's deception of her and her anxiety for the future. She had borne an illegitimate child and because of this had lost her character. She had spent all her savings and had no more money. She would need to go back into domestic service. 'To her disordered mind, apparently the death of West and herself appeared the only termination to an intolerable situation.'

Crosby clearly considered that at the time of the killing Alice was suffering great emotional strain. No wonder, I say to myself. Her experience of labour and birth would be traumatic for any woman, then or now. It explained so much of her behaviour at this time. The travails of childbirth, its messiness and pain, were women's concerns and seldom discussed in public. Alice may not even have talked much of her experience once she left the nursing home. It was easier now to see the causes of her mounting desperation. For her serious crime Chief Justice Robert Stout had locked Alice up for a lifetime, but, ironically, the hardest labour of her sentence was undergone before her trial and even before Bert West was slain.

ELEVEN

With Hard Labour — the play

Once more back in Nelson, I gathered my notes and memories together to work out how I was going to write this play. It was an ordinary people's story and so must be full of voices. Alice's parents, George and Isabella, would be there and her lawyers, friends, bystanders, shopkeepers, other prisoners, women's groups, warders and unionists would all be heard — but Alice's voice must be the clearest of all. In all these years she had not had a chance to speak for herself, but in this play she would take centre stage. The piece would end with her coming out of gaol. I had not managed to find any of Alice's descendants, so I knew nothing of her life after that.

I decided to start the play with Alice in her cell when she first arrived at Addington Reformatory. She would be uncooperative and almost despairing. I typed the first few words. They were from MATRON MCBRYDE, who barked: 'Parkinson, you're going to be here for a long time so you might as well make the best of it. You're a clean, healthy girl by all accounts, and a strong one ...' and the play begins.

Some plays almost write themselves, as this one did. I included Salvation Army hymns and popular songs of the day, newspaper advertisements, court records, gaol scenes and protest rallies. By November the play was finished and was kindly workshopped by Dr John Dawick at Massey University in Palmerston North.[1] The day-long workshop took the form of a rehearsed reading and a discussion of the play to follow. To make the experience more interesting for those taking part we borrowed costumes from the nearby Globe Theatre in Main Street, and my father measured out and painted SAVE ALICE PARKINSON in large black letters on a long white cloth banner that we used in the eventual production of the play. After the workshop I tidied up the writing and, as suggested, entered *With Hard Labour* into the Adam Foundation Playwriting Competition. The play got into the finals and I was overjoyed, primarily because this gave it a better chance of being staged.

Phillip Mann, the Wellington writer, university lecturer and theatre director, had been a judge for the Adam awards. He agreed to direct *With Hard Labour,* along with a local Nelson director, the secondary schoolteacher and theatre director Jo Kahl. Now a core group of friendly and capable Nelson women came together to help stage the play. At the home of one of these stalwart women we did another reading, arranged a venue for auditions and booked the Suter Theatre (alongside the Suter Art Gallery in Nelson) for November. The new play was on its way.

Gradually the roles available in the play were taken up by Nelson people. Fiona Sills, a young Nelson woman, was to play Alice. We started rehearsals at a barn-like inner city arts centre. It was a great space for theatre. Phil Mann came across from Wellington as often as possible to guide and direct the actors. Slowly, the play was taking shape. We needed a poster to advertise the coming performances and Janice Gill offered to create one. In the black-and-white poster Alice is impassively looking outwards. In front of her are vertical black bars with one painted across the right side of her face. Behind her is a stylised wooden cottage of the period. The two posts of its verandah are the wooden posts of the Parkinson house that Janice had sketched at Tikokino the previous year. We were to use this striking image of Alice on all of our advertising notices, programmes and tickets.

Soon, opening night was just days away and Phil Mann suggested that I have one last try to find any members of Alice's family who might have wished to see the play. Accordingly, I wrote out a brief notice stating that *With Hard Labour*, a play about Alice May Parkinson, was to be performed in Nelson in November and that anyone interested could contact me via my

Nelson phone number. I placed this notice in leading newspapers in Auckland, Wellington, Christchurch and Dunedin, but nobody replied. Then, perhaps two days before the play was to go on I got a phone call. A man's voice asked, 'Have you got anything to do with this play about Alice Parkinson?' 'Yes,' I said, and asked if he was any relation of Alice's. He said, 'I ought to be, I'm her son.' And my heart turned over.

Raymond O'Loughlin told me that he just happened to see my advertisement by chance, among the back pages of the Auckland paper. He told one of his brothers about it and said 'Should we go to see the play?' but his older brother said 'No. If it comes to Auckland, we'll go along and sit at the back.' Nevertheless, Ray himself was keen to come. He would travel down from Auckland by bus and ferry the next day and I would meet him at the Nelson bus depot. Now I was less nervous about opening night than I was about how Ray would take the play. What would it mean to him to see his mother portrayed on stage? She was not just a 'character' made up from my imagination. She was a real and suffering human being. Not for the first time I realised the responsibility I had to be fair and true to the people I put on stage.

When Ray stepped off the bus we went for a coffee and a long talk. He said he was one of six children, so I discovered that Alice was eventually able to go on and have a family. He had not had an easy childhood and never really knew what had happened to his mother, only that it was something wrapped in secrecy and very bad. Ray told me that his mother Alice (known as 'May') always suffered from severe headaches. I thought of the bullet in her head and knew why.

The next time I saw Ray it was opening night at the Suter Theatre. He sat beside me and watched, largely in silence, as the story of his mother unfolded. Afterwards, the excited cast were happy and relieved that the play had gone well, and Ray wanted to come back and see it for another time before he got on the bus on the long trip back to Auckland. The next night he sat beside me again and watched silently. At the end of the performance Fiona

Sills, who was playing Alice, came out on her own to the front of the stage and said that tonight we had a very special guest. She told the audience that Alice's son was here with us. The whole audience stood up and turned around to where we were sitting and applauded warmly. I looked at Ray. There were tears running down his cheeks. It is hard to describe that moment.

Alice and Charles O'Loughlin with two of their children, 1930.

Four O'Loughlin children: Yvonne, Bryan, Ray and Norman (with an unknown woman at the rear).

Ray wrote to me several times after that and I wrote back. He had gone home with a video of the play and a copy of an academic essay I had written on Alice's case for Massey University.[2] After a playwrights' conference in Auckland in December he picked me up in his car and drove me to the airport, and before my flight we sat in a café and talked some more. I could never give to Ray on stage his mother as she actually was; nobody could do that, but perhaps in the play Fiona Sills and I had given him a version of his mother's experience that might help him to understand her more.

TWELVE

Finding Jennie

Jennie and I did not have the easiest of introductions. It was 2002, and Colin and I were packing up and clearing our Nelson house to travel to the Solomon Islands where we would live and work for the next two years. We had promised to be out of the house by the next day. The tenant who would live in it while we were away was anxious to be there at the earliest time possible and would move in as soon as we were gone. There were boxes everywhere and there was so much work still to do. In the midst of this chaos I got a phone call. It was from Jennie O'Loughlin, who told me she was Alice's granddaughter. She had only recently discovered who her grandmother was. Could she come and talk to me about her? It was already afternoon by now. I looked around at the suitcases and boxes. It was the busiest day of my life and I was beyond tired.

'No,' I said, 'I'm really sorry. I'm packing up to get out of this house and I just don't have any time left.' It was ironic that I had tried to find members of Alice's family, and now, when a granddaughter had unexpectedly found me, I had no time to talk to her.

And that was where it stayed. We went away overseas and eventually settled back again in New Zealand. And then, in 2012, I got another call from Jennie. She and her partner had a bar and café down at Franz Josef. They had named it the Alice May, in memory of her grandmother. Jennie asked me if I could send her a DVD of *With Hard Labour.* I had only a video copy, filmed mostly at a rehearsal, but a 'techie' friend at Massey put this on to a DVD for me and I sent it to Jennie. A little later I had another call. What she would have really liked was a book about Alice —

to learn more about her and to bring into the light rather than hide away her grandmother's life and experience.

I mulled over this for a while. I had spent so much time over the years searching for, thinking about and writing about Alice Parkinson. Somehow, in a strange kind of way, she was part of my life too. In the end I emailed Jennie to say I would write the book.

And here it is. This book has been written especially for Jennie, but it is also for Ray, who came down from Auckland to see the play, and for George and Isabella Parkinson who gave Alice such unstinting love and care throughout all of her tribulations.

So many notable individuals walk through these pages of Alice's history — lawyer Barney Dolan, poet and reformer Blanche Baughan, labour leader Harry Holland, campaigner Clara Rae, unionist Jane Donaldson and, yes, even Chief Justice Sir Robert Stout, but Alice's story is also a celebration of all of the ordinary people who fought for her as well. All those carpenters, housewives, soldiers, ministers, nurses, builders and shopworkers who filled the halls, wrote the letters to *Truth*, signed the petitions, raised the money, pressured the government and by doing so never let her be forgotten. This book is for them too.

Notes

Part One

Introduction

1. J T B Todd, letter to *Truth*, 10 April 1920, p 2.

1 A bright and cheerful Christian

1. For material on early Hampden (now known as Tikokino) see Sally Butler and Judy Matthews, *Tikokino A History 1855–1990*, Waipukarau, 1991.
2. The school was not officially renamed Tikokino School until 1908.
3. Edith Amy Todd, from a letter dated 15 March 1920, probably to the Prisons Board. The Todds had known Alice when she was in service in Hastings and were fellow Salvation Army members and friends.

2 Napier

1. *Truth*, 1 May 1915, p 4.
2. *ibid*
3. In the records of the day Forde's name is spelt both with and without a final 'e'. The Napier electoral roll has *Forde*.
4. *Truth*, 1 May 1915, p 4.
5. J. Acc. W 2636 Box 2 1915/256, National Archives.
6. *ibid*
7. Unposted letters to Mary Ann West, *Truth*, 1 May 1915, p 4.

3 Confrontation

1. *Truth*, 1 May 1915, p 4 (Margaret Innes)
2. *ibid*
3. *ibid*
4. *ibid*
5. *ibid*
6. *Truth*, 24 April, p 9.
7. J 46 Coroner's Court records, 1915/486, National Archives.

4 Aftermath

1. *Truth*, 1 May 1915, p 4.

5 Trial

1. Taken from trial records J Acc. W Box 2 1915/256, National Archives.
2. The jurymen were J E Wilson (foreman); J Ball; P Farquhar; A A Vickerstaff; A H Burr; S Thornton; W Watson; A J Williamson; P McDonald; J A Burtenshaw; G R Stevens; A J Turvelle.
3. *Daily Telegraph,* Napier, 9 June 1915, p 6.
4. Baby farmers were paid to take in and care for unwanted infants(most of them illegitimate). The shame surrounding 'bastard' children at this time meant that trafficking or 'farming' children in this way was normally done with great secrecy. Minnie Dean, still remembered as 'the Winton baby farmer', was charged with child murder when several of the infants in her care were found to have died. In 1895 she went to her death still protesting her innocence. She became the only woman to be hanged by law in New Zealand.
5. Trial evidence, J. Acc. W Box 2 1915/256, National Archives.
6. *ibid*
7. *Truth,* 19 June 1915, p 7.
8. *ibid*
9. *ibid*
10. Rex v Parkinson, Gazette Law Reports, Vol. xvii, August 20 1915, pp 533–534.

6 Addington

1. J. Acc. W Box 2 1915/256, N A.
2. Lock Hospital: See Sandra Coney, *Standing in the Sunshine: A History of New Zealand Women Since they Won the Vote.* Auckland: Penguin Books (NZ), 1993, p 122.
3. Personal communication, Bronwyn Dalley, 14 May 1992. For an account of early Addington Prison see also David Gee, *The Devil's Own Brigade: A History of the Lyttelton Gaol 1860–1920,* Wellington: Millward Press, 1975.

7 Protest

1. *Truth,* 26 June 1915, p 6.
2. *Truth,* 10 July 1915, p 5.
3. *ibid*
4. The Social Democratic Party was the political arm and the United Federation of Labour the industrial arm of the growing New Zealand labour movement. The two groups were to merge in July 1916 to form the New Zealand Labour Party.
5. The members of the steering committee were Messrs G L Rae, J Glover, Harry Holland and Mesdames Rae, Hickey and Snow.
6. *Maoriland Worker,* 28 July 1915, p 4.
7. *ibid*
8. Clara E Rae, a long-term campaigner for Alice's cause.

9. *Maoriland Worker,* 21 July 1915, p 3.
10. *ibid,* 4 August 1915, p 4.
11. Joseph Pawelka was a Manawatu thief and outlaw. In 1910 he had been controversially pronounced a habitual criminal and sentenced to 21 years' imprisonment. The harshness of this sentence caused a considerable outcry from the public. In 1912 Pawelka escaped from the Terrace Gaol in Wellington. He was never recaptured.
12. *Maoriland Worker,* 4 August 1915, p 4.
13. 'Release Alice Parkinson' Women's Meeting, *ibid.* Jane Donaldson, appointed Secretary of the Release Alice Parkinson Campaign at this meeting, was an English suffragette who arrived in New Zealand in 1912 and became active in the Social Democratic Party and in the Housewives' League. She was to be an untiring fighter for Alice's freedom.
14. *Evening Post,* 12 August 1915, p 2.
15. Letter to the Women's Christian Temperance Union magazine *White Ribbon,* 18 August 1915, p 7.
16. For accounts of this Wellington Town Hall meeting see *Maoriland Worker,* 22 September 1915, p 4 and *Evening Post,* 17 September 1915, p 5.
17. *Maoriland Worker,* 21 October 1915, p 7.
18. *Truth,* 31 July 1915, p 5: 'A Soldier's Tribute'
19. *ibid*: An Offer of Marriage'
20. *Truth,* 23 October 1915, p 8.

8 Despair

1. *Truth* headlines, 2 September 1916, p 5.
2. Stout was president of the Anti-Chinese League. See Roberta Nicholls' entry on Anna Stout (Robert Stout's wife) in *The Book of New Zealand Women: Ko Kui Ma Te Kaupapa,*. Eds. Charlotte Macdonald, Merimeri Penfold and Bridget Williams, Wellington: Bridget Williams Books, 1991, p 634.
3. Waldo Dunn & Ivor Richardson, *Sir Robert Stout,* Wellington: A H & A W Reed, 1961, p 177.
4. New Zealand Parliamentary Debates, Vol.55, 23 June 1886, p 70.
5. *Truth,* 2 September 1916, p 5.
6. Journals of the New Zealand House of Representatitves Public Petitions M to Z Committee, July, 1916. Clara E Rae and others. This is not the large petition organised by *Truth.* It is separate.
7. 'Alice Parkinson's Present Home' letter from Annie Jones to *Truth,* 10 July 1915, p 5.
8. Jane Donaldson, letter to *Truth,* 22 June 1918, p 2.
9. *Truth,* 16 June 1917, p 6.
10. *ibid*
11. J. Acc. W Box 2 1915/256 National Archives
12. Captain Belle Parkinson was now living at Kaiapoi, near Christchurch, and as a concession she was permitted to visit her sister in gaol, although these

visits were allowed only on the basis that they might be cancelled if Alice's behaviour worsened.

13. A letter from an overworked mother, 'Ex-Employer', says in part: 'She resided with me for some time as help. I have had many excellent servants in my time but I have always affirmed that I liked Alice Parkinson best of any. She was affectionate with my children, and quiet and industrious in household matters, and showed absolute consideration and kindness towards me', *Truth,* 17 July 1915, p 5. There are other letters in similar vein.
14. Blanche Baughan went on to found the Howard League for Penal Reform in Christchurch in 1924. For more on her life see Nancy Harris's essay in the *Dictionary of New Zealand Biography* Vol.3 1901–1920, Auckland: AUP & BWB, 1996, pp 38–39.
15. These two runaways were most likely from the Te Oranga Reformatory for Delinquent Women in Burwood, Christchurch.
16. J. Acc. W Box 2 1915/256 National Archives
17. Judith Allen, *Sex and Secrets: Crimes Involving Australian Women Since 1880,* Melbourne: Oxford University Press, 1990, pp 81–82.

9 The free air of God's own country

1. *Truth,* 12 April 1919, p 5
2. *ibid*
3. The minutes of this group are held in the Alexander Turnbull Library
4. *Maoriland Worker,* 18 February 1920, p 7
5. *Auckland Star*, 28 June 1920, p 6
6. The Alice Parkinson Release Committee campaigners were J Jeffrey (chairman), E Stevenson (secretary) and H Woodroff, organiser of the big Globe Theatre meeting in Auckland.
7. J Acc. W2636 Box 2 1915/256 National Archives
8. *ibid*
9. *ibid*
10. *ibid*
11. *ibid*
12. *ibid*
13. *ibid*
14. *ibid*
15. Redmer Yska, Truth: The rise and fall of the people's paper. Nelson: Craig Potton Publishing, 2010, p 55.
16. *Truth* 3 September, p 5

Part Two

10 Finding Alice

1. Carol Markwell, *Save Our Railway,* A community play, 1991.
2. *The People and the Land Te Tangata me Te Whenua: An Illustrated History of New Zealand 1820–1920*. Eds. Judith Bassett, Judith Binney and Erik Olssen, Wellington: Allen & Unwin, 1990.
3. This was Beryl Parkinson, second wife of one of Alice's brothers. She died in 1997.
4. She will later paint a picture from one of these street scenes. 'I'm One of Mrs Shipley's Children, Eh?/ Colonisation' (1993). The picture is reprinted in Janice Gill's *Telling Stories,* Wellington: Steele Roberts, 2009, p 131.
5. J Acc. W Box 2 1915/256 National Archives.

11 *With Hard Labour* — the play

1. Throughout this time I was an extramural student at Massey University, studying English, History and Drama.
2. *The Case of Alice Parkinson: Its Social and Political Context,* Diploma of Humanities research essay, 1993.

Appendix: 'A Woman Wronged'

The poem sent anonymously to Truth newpaper — see page 58.

"Being by way of comment on the harsh sentence imposed on Alice Parkinson, the young woman sentenced to imprisonment for the term of her natural life for shooting her false lover.

Scorned by the man whose babe I bore,
Who left me outcast, neither maid nor wife;
On whom I'd blindly spent my scanty store.
Fondly believing I should share his life;
Desperate, distraught, half mad with grief and shame,
I shot that man — was I to blame?

Blinded by love, I suffered each rebuff,
Foolishly thinking love would grow again;
By kith and kin abhorred, my path was rough,
But little cared I, buoyed by love's fierce flame.
When disillusion came — a dark day dawned.
Hell has no fury like a woman scorned.

And then that man-made law which men call just,
That law unsentimental, uninspired,
Opened its ponderous tomes all thick with dust,
And on me wreaked the vengeance it desired.
In gaol I have to languish all my life.
Oh, pity me:— a mother but no wife."

The poem came with a handwritten note: *"Cannot you Sir use your influence that God Almighty has placed in your hands to have the sentence on this unfortunate woman reduced."*

References

While researching Alice's story I consulted too many references to be able to include all of them in this list. Here are some of the more readily obtainable ones if you would like to read more. Each of these items has been a useful source for my text.

Books

Allen, Judith. *Sex & Secrets: crimes involving Australian women since 1880.* Melbourne: Oxford University Press, 1990

Bassett, Judith, Judith Binney and Erik Olssen, eds, *The people and the Land / Te tangata me te whenua: an illustrated history of New Zealand, 1820–1920.* Wellington: Allen & Unwin, 1990

Butler, Sally and Judy Matthews. *Tikokino: A History, 1855–1990.* Tikokino: Tikokino School Jubilee Book Committee, 1991

Coney, Sandra. *Standing in the Sunshine: A History of New Zealand women since they won the vote.* Auckland: Penguin Books, 1993

Dictionary of New Zealand Biography, The Vol. 3 1901–1920. Auckland: Auckland University Press, 1996. (This is now also online — Te Ara 2011)

Dunn, Waldo and Ivor Richardson. *Sir Robert Stout: a biography.* Wellington: A H & A W Reed, 1961

Gee, David. *The Devil's Own Brigade: A History of Lyttelton Gaol, 1860–1920.* Wellington: Millward Press, 1975

Macdonald, Charlotte, Merimeri Penfold and Bridget Williams, eds. *The Book of New Zealand Women.* Wellington: Bridget Williams Books, 1991

Yska, Redmer. *Truth: the rise and fall of the people's paper.* Nelson: Craig Potton Publishing, 2010

Articles

Dalley, Bronwyn. 'Prisons without men: the development of a separate women's prison in New Zealand.' *New Zealand Journal of History* 27, No 1 (1993): 37–60

Hamer, David. 'Sir Robert Stout' in *New Zealand's Heritage*, vol. 50 (1971): 1391–1396

Robinson, Jan. 'Canterbury's rowdy women: whores, madonnas and female criminality.' *NZ Women's Studies Journal* 1, No 1 (1984): 6–25

Newspapers and journals

Auckland Star, 1920

Evening Post, 1915–1920

Maoriland Worker, 1915–1921

Truth, 1915–1921

White Ribbon, 1907–1918

Journals of the House of Representatives, Report of the Petitions Committee M–Z, 1916

New Zealand Government Gazette, 1915

New Zealand Parliamentary Debates, 1886–1920

Minute books

Auckland Women's International and Political League minute books 1917–1925, Alexander Turnbull Library, Wellington

Index